AMERICA'S
YOUNGEST
HOSTAGES

IAN KELDOULIS

AMERICA'S YOUNGEST HOSTAGES

THE TRUE COST OF FOSTER CARE
AND WHO'S PAYING FOR IT

AMERICA'S YOUNGEST HOSTAGES
The True Cost of Foster Care and Who's Paying for It

Cover Design: Rafael Andres

Text design: meadencreative.com

First Edition 2019

Hardcover: 978-0-9996572-2-5

Paperback: 978-0-9996572-3-2

eBook: 978-0-9996572-4-9

Contents

Preface

This book was born from two contradictory emotions: celebration and frustration.

Downey Side, an independent adoption agency, has been working tirelessly to find permanent homes for America's neediest children for half a century. The origins of this book lie in the celebration of the agency's golden anniversary. With over seven thousand success stories, there is a lot to be happy about.

However, Downey Side sadly finds itself fighting the same problems today as it did back in 1967, when the agency was founded. The foster-care system hasn't evolved. At any given time, approximately half a million American children are suffering in foster-care limbo. It is a self-perpetuating monster that fails daily to serve the best interests of children. Our foster-care system is designed to fuel the large US pipeline of child institutionalization. We would like the system to disappear.

The goal of this book is to generate awareness about *America's Youngest Hostages* and to inspire systemic change that frees them from a broken system. To do this, I have drawn from Downey Side's extensive experience in child services. Together with the agency, we are channeling our frustration into the energy needed to help foster-care children find a better way.

Real change is long overdue. Reforms to the foster-care system can't happen at a glacial pace because we are dealing with the lives and futures of children. *Urgent* reform is needed.

We chose the title *America's Youngest Hostages* because it provocatively describes the true situation of many children. The book was written to educate average Americans, people who probably have no knowledge of child welfare services. To end the deplorable foster-care system, regular folk need to hear the message of this book. We hope more will be enraged enough to take action.

We also want the book to encourage other adoption agencies and child advocates to work together on this massive problem. If this book inspires more partnerships and collaboration, that will be another reason to celebrate.

Author's Note

I'm not an expert in child welfare. So, why have I written about foster care? Well, the tremendous work of the Downey Side adoption agency, a small organization with an outsized passion, has inspired me.

In short, I wrote the book because I wanted to fight with David against Goliath. The foster-care system is huge. It determines the lives of about half a million children. By contrast, Downey Side has a few small offices scattered across a couple of states. Downey Side alone would never have the means to empty the foster-care system through adoption. Yet the overwhelming odds has never stopped them from trying. Every child out of the system is a child saved.

Father Paul Engel's passion to save children and his animosity toward the foster-care system has kept him fighting for fifty years. As the founder of Downey Side, Father Paul is still hoping for that miraculous sling-shot hit between the eyes that will take the system down.

Under Father Paul's leadership, Downey Side has remained a classic grassroots organization. It has stayed true to its mission of finding permanent families for the most intractably stuck children in foster care—older children, sibling groups, and children with difficulties.

Writing about Downey Side's story is important to me. If people wait for this huge problem to solve itself, nothing will happen. The hard-working Downey Side community of families and supporters is not waiting. I have experienced their joy and sense of purpose. They have inspired me to write about a very troubling topic.

Father Paul is also inspirational. Although I'm not a religious person, or perhaps because I'm not, he has had a big impact on my life. Our politics often don't align. But we have found common cause across political lines, and that feels like an important act. If people can't come together to help children in dire need, what does that say about us?

This book doesn't claim to have all the solutions to the problems of child welfare in America. It does, however, show how a small organization with ton of passion can inspire a community. And if community after community becomes concerned, change will happen. It will happen in a way that people can readily understand and see for themselves.

The huge problem of foster care reaches into the heart of how we understand family. The recent debate over immigration has drawn attention to the harm that family separation causes children. Yet, the same thing is happening to hundreds of thousands of American children every year under the auspices of foster care with very little media attention.

Foster care has to end. If this book can shine a light on the terrible suffering hidden all around us, then it will be a success. If it inspires people to take action, it will be a triumph.

Foreword

I see the hand of God in my journey. He seems to have worked through Father Paul Engel, a man who changed my life. Without him, I never would have become a Capuchin friar or a special education teacher. I never would have spent three decades serving people in Guam.

That's because Father Paul found a permanent home for me when I was young. And that family stability was my foundation.

Perhaps I had a positive affect on him too. I was the first person he helped escape institutionalization. Would this young priest have founded Downey Side adoption agency and helped thousands of children break free from foster care for more than half a century if I hadn't come along?

My biological father was a religious and educated man, a pharmaceutical salesman who had briefly studied medicine. But everything fell apart shortly after he had a sixth child with my mother. She left us. My grandparents were elderly and couldn't help. All of this was too much for my father to handle. He tried his best, but under the strain he reached for the bottle. I was about three-years old.

Uncertain of what to do, he brought all of his kids to the Brightside orphanage. The orphanage immediately split us up and housed us in separate buildings. When that approach failed, my two oldest brothers stayed with my father, my two sisters went to an aunt, and my youngest brother went to a family known by my father. I bounced around.

Eventually, I went back to my father and oldest brothers. We were unsupervised, except on Sundays when my father took us to Mass. He used to tell me, "You're God's disciple on the weekends, and the devil's disciple during the week."

At age sixteen, while returning home on a bus from my dishwashing job, I thought, "What's going to happen to me?" I was fresh out of reform school with a history of shoplifting. I had no education beyond eighth grade. I could barely read. Home was a rooming house, shared with my older brother, in downtown Springfield, Massachusetts.

The Capuchins had a chapel there. I got off the bus, went in to pray, and confessed. That's when I met Father Paul.

In the chapel, Father Paul took me aside and asked me some questions. He wanted to know where I lived and what I did. Discovering that my mother was gone and that my father was incapable of parenting, he asked if I knew anyone he could talk to about me? I had a good friend whose father was a heart specialist. His family (they had eight children) liked me and often fed me. So Father Paul went to see them.

The family's neighbor was a single lady, Margaret Downey. Father Paul went next door and asked her if she would take me in. I don't know why, but she did. Although she never formally adopted me, she was a real mother—a godsend.

Margaret told me she had never met the right man. At fifty-eight, she was living in a Victorian house with four bedrooms, three fireplaces, two bathrooms, and a staircase framed by stained glass. Her good friend who shared the home was dying in hospital. Margaret and I developed a deep and permanent bond.

I wanted to become a priest, but my lack of education made that dream impossible. However, Father Paul told me I could become a friar. So, when I turned eighteen, I entered the friary.

Margret knew my decision was like "saying goodbye to the world." She was determined to show me the world first. She booked us both a trip to Europe on the Queen Mary. We went to England, Ireland, and Rome. Her friends thought she was crazy for spending so much money. But upon our return, she learned that a relative had died and left her $5,000, which more than paid for our trip. Like so many things with her, that provision was evidence to me of God's work.

In 1980, I moved to Guam, where I served in numerous ministries and eventually started teaching fourth grade. I stayed with Margaret during all of my return trips. When she was fatally ill with kidney disease, I returned to look after her as much as I could. I participated in her funeral in 1999.

How would my life have turned out if Father Paul hadn't placed me with Margaret Downey? It's impossible to say. But I know my odds would not have been good.

Downey Side, named after Margaret, has been the life's work of Father Paul. That he and his team have placed thousands of older children like me into permanent families is a true measure of success. But that's just the beginning.

The stability I found with Margaret enabled me to serve many other people. When you magnify the help Father Paul and Margaret gave me by several thousand others whom Downey Side has helped, and when you think about all the people they have helped, what you get is a better society.

This book does more than tell the story of Downey Side and Father Paul. It's really about the importance of family. However a family is structured, permanence and commitment are what children and adolescents need most. Unfortunately, today's foster-care system doesn't provide permanence or commitment. It is no better than the system I experienced half a century ago. It's still a pipeline to prison for many who have done nothing other than find themselves in a bad situation.

I'm grateful that Ian Keldoulis has written a book for people who don't understand the trauma of foster care or the child welfare system. When you read this book, you'll hear the call for change loud and clear.

Ultimately, my life was changed by a simple act: Getting off a bus instead of continuing my usual journey. It's my hope that reading *America's Youngest Hostages* will inspire you to take a simple step with tremendous consequences—joining the fight to end foster care.

Br. Brian Champoux, O.F.M. Cap.

Chapter One

A Life Sentence

What follows is the account of a young man who grew up in the Texas foster-care system. He was a Downey Side adoptee. I call him Timothy, but his name is withheld to protect his privacy.

I was five-years old when my dad, after lashing me with his belt, hit me over the head with a beer bottle. He went to jail. I was sentenced, too. I went into foster care.

Over the next three-and-a-half years, I was in six different foster homes. I was sexually abused. I was forced to eat food off the floor as punishment. Nobody bothered to teach me the basics of personal hygiene; I didn't learn how to properly brush my teeth, comb my hair, or bathe. I never knew how long I would stay in the same place. The last home I lived in, when escape finally became a possibility, was strictly business. I was their source of income, along with seven other children.

Picture a home with eight children living in it. What do you see and hear? Kids running and playing, toys on the floor, crayon drawings covering the fridge, crying, laughter. Right?

Wrong. My last place had four boys and four girls in two different rooms. We had separate bathrooms, which we had to clean ourselves. The system classified each of us as "special needs" kids, which meant that we were worth more money to the foster parents. We were all heavily medicated. I was on four different psychotropic drugs. The dosages were better suited to a forty-year-old person. The result? I was so drugged up that I couldn't play—even if there had been toys to play with. People who won't buy an eight-year old a toothbrush don't typically spend money on toys or help you with your ABCs. The drugs kept us all asleep most of the time.

When my adoptive parents came to visit, they knew immediately this was no place for happy children. It was a human warehouse. It's difficult to describe how it feels to be treated this way, but it's easy to see the effect it had on me. I was diagnosed as depressed and emotionally disturbed. Officially, I had Oppositional Defiance Disorder, Post-Traumatic Stress Disorder, and Attention Deficit Hyperactive Disorder. It's a wonder my adoptive parents could take me on.

These "mental diseases" were just symptoms. In the past, people would have described me as an angry, undisciplined, tormented, and neglected child who acted out emotionally. And they'd be right. The underlying "disease" or "cause" is obvious: I didn't have a family who loved me.

Today there's an entire industry built around people like me. It's hidden in plain sight behind medical terminology, layers of bureaucracy, and walls of silence. Some folks call it the "foster-care industrial complex." We just call it "the system." The longer you're in the system, the harder it is to escape. After all, who wants to take on a deeply troubled teenager?

If you can think of a way to neglect a human being, it happens in the system. The neglect occurs during a child's most formative years. Because I was so drugged up, learning anything at school was more or less impossible. There was nobody at home who cared whether I was doing my homework or classwork. I learned that miserable personal hygiene doesn't win friends. I was a social outcast, which was painful, and I couldn't even trust the people I lived with; but daily survival was more important to me than social life. Survival involved learning how to hoard basic necessities and to forego attachments.

Through it all, I learned that my value as a human being was defined by my place in the system. I was the widget that got traded and shipped. Or I was the system's currency for foster parents, social workers, doctors, and bureaucrats. Everything about me had a price—my age, the number of siblings I had, the problems I had acquired, and the amount of time that I had been in the system. All of those factors made me worth more, or less.

And I could hear the system's clock ticking. I knew that the older I got the less likely I would be adopted. Everyone wants cute. Everyone wants a blank slate. And as my case file began to overflow with problems, I could feel my value shift. I knew that people were making money because of me.

It's tempting to say it all ended when I was finally adopted. After years of dashed hopes, with one potential adoption after another turning to dust, I did make it out of the system. A family in New York took me home, away from my last foster placement in Texas, and into a new life.

However, like all children in the system, I couldn't just leave my past behind. My formative years had been total chaos. I had grown up with no stability or control over my life. Foster care had extracted a heavy toll deep within me.

The first thing my new parents did was get me off the drugs. Their pharmacist was stunned by the massive amounts of medication I was on and recommended hospitalization while I was detoxing. Getting off drugs had consequences. In my case, the main purpose of the drugs was to bottle my emotions. You can guess what happened when they locked up the medications. It wasn't pretty.

My adoptive mother bore the brunt of it. I would scream, "I hate you! I hate you! I hate you!" for an hour and a half. Then, because I had never been parented, I would refuse to go to bed. In response, she wouldn't let me watch TV and turned off the light. That led to more screaming for another hour or so. I acted like that for a couple of years.

She knew that my anger wasn't directed at her, but that didn't make it easier for her to endure the abuse. We both knew that I found it hard to trust her, or anybody. I struggled to accept that my birth mom had abandoned me. Why would she do that? What was wrong with me?

So, I unleashed my anger on the nearest mother available. Everything that had been bottled up exploded around her. I compensated for my youthful lack of vocabulary with emotional intensity.

On the other hand, I couldn't leave my new mother alone. Every time she turned around, I was there. I hovered so close that she would accidentally knock me in the head with her elbow all the time. I stayed close because I was desperate to be held and loved. So, our conversations were conflicted. "I hate you." "I love you." "I trust you." "I don't trust you." "I need you." "I don't need you." "I love you." "Fuck you!" That type of relationship went on for a long time. Internally, I was a vacuum.

*****

My life in foster care began when I was living with my birth mom and three siblings. We lived in the back of a mechanic's garage. Child protective services got involved and separated us. I wound up with my biological dad. When that went sour, I landed in foster care.

After about seventeen years of separation, I went back to visit my birth family. Desperate for answers, I pressured my adoptive parents to give me a ticket to Texas. They bought my ticket as a birthday present.

When I arrived Texas, I got answers, but not the ones I was looking for. I never found a concrete reason for why I had been abandoned. My mother hadn't been on death's door or anything like that. So, I simply don't have answers. There is no "closure." Nothing is resolved. So, I learned to refocus, and I moved toward future happiness. I'm thankful to have a close relationship with one of my siblings.

The profoundly sad thing about my story is not the neglect, abuse, and suffering. It's that my story is so *common*—at least in part. Unlike many people raised in the system, my story has a happy ending. I have a good life at age twenty-two: a job, a car, people who care about me. I'm dating. Life is not without its problems, but my permanent family gave me opportunities. But that's not how a lot of kids in foster care wind up.

For many people like me, foster care is just the *beginning* of an institutionalized life. The system isn't set up for the benefit of the children in it. Our jails are loaded with former foster kids. Some kids age out and get on with their lives, but the odds are heavily stacked against them.

We need to change those odds. We need to change the system.

The story of Timothy McAdam*, Downey Side Adoptee, as told to Ian Keldoulis.

*Name changed for reasons of privacy.

Chapter Two

Welcome to the Machine

"Every child has the right to a permanent, legal family."

Father Paul Engel, O.F.M. Cap., Founder of Downey Side, Adoption Agency.

Human beings don't cope with uncertainty very well. We're not wired for it. It stresses us. Knowing that a train is coming in five minutes makes the wait easier to endure than staring down a dark tunnel wondering, *How long now?* That's why subway systems around the world spend millions of dollars on indicator boards. The signs don't make the trains come any faster, but they keep passengers calm.

Kids in foster care grow up gazing down a dark tunnel. There are no signs. After the system separates them from their birth parents, they long for attachment and stability. They want to go *home*. Not just a physical place, but a home where they are loved. To a family. It may never come. And any indication that a permanent home is approaching soon usually turns out to be unreliable. This constant anxiety has devastating effects for children.

Children go into foster care if their safety is considered to be at risk. The government removes them from their homes to protect them from neglect and abuse. In Timothy's case, the final straw occurred when his father hit him over the head with a bottle. In theory, the foster-care system is supposed to return children to their original parents when the abuse and neglect issues have been resolved. But such problems are often intractable. The courts sent Timothy's father to jail. His mother ultimately gave up four of her five children. Once the state terminates the birth parent's rights, an alternative permanent home for the child has to be found.

The theory of foster care as a temporary solution rarely works. In practice, it's often a perpetual state of legal limbo in which a child's guardianship is handed over to the state for an indefinite period of time. As the child ages, the chances of getting out of the system diminish. The longer a child spends in the system, the more his or her problems will compound.

Timothy's story illustrates the typical trajectory of a child in the foster-care system. Shuffled from home to home, foster parents treat ever-increasing emotional problems with medication. This leaves the child inadequately prepared for the day when he or she is ejected from the system into society. Had Timothy stayed in foster care, there's a good chance he would have ended up in jail.

The University of Chicago[1] studied youth who had been in foster care at age seventeen—to see how they had fared by age twenty-three. More than two out of five young men with foster-care history (42.8 percent) had been convicted of a crime as an adult. As for men who had not been in the foster-care system, less than one out of ten had committed crimes.

Life improves for youth in foster care when they find permanent parents with a legally binding stake in the child's future. That

[1] Mark E. Courtney, et al., Midwest Evaluation of the Adult Functioning of Former Foster Youth: Outcomes at Ages 23 and 24 (Chapin Hall Center for Children at the University of Chicago, 2010).

was certainly the case for Timothy. At last, he gained real permanency and security.

Most people don't know that foster parents are not legal guardians. So, the true legal guardian is the governor of the state in which the child lives. Having thousands of public servants between a child and his or her legal parents is not the recipe for raising emotionally healthy children.

When the system functions at its worst, poor oversight leads to rampant abuse. That problem came to light in a class-action case by a group of children who had been placed in the Texas foster-care system (*Stukenberg v. Abbott*[2]). After the federal district court in Corpus Christi ruled that the Fourteenth Amendment rights of the children had been systematically violated, the *Dallas Observer* called the system a "state-sponsored rape factory." On December 17, 2015, after 254 pages of testimony and findings, Senior United States District Judge Janis Graham Jack said the following:

> *Texas's foster-care system is broken, and it has been that way for decades. It is broken for all stakeholders, including DFPS (Department of Family Protective Services) employees who are tasked with impossible workloads. Most importantly, though, it is broken for Texas's PMC (Permanent Managing Conservatorship) children, who almost uniformly leave State custody more damaged than when they entered. … The reality is that DFPS has ignored twenty years of reports, outlining problems and recommending solutions. DFPS has also ignored professional standards. All the while, Texas's PMC children have been shuttled throughout a system*

---

[2] Stukenberg, *et al.*,Plaintiffs, vs. Greg Abott, *et al.*, Defendants. United States District Court Southern District of Texas, CIVIL ACTION NO. 2:11-CV-84 Entered December 17, 2015, David J. Bradley, Clerk

*where rape, abuse, psychotropic medication, and
instability are the norm.*

Across the country, the system is plagued with problems. Days after the Texas ruling, New York City Public Advocate[3] Letitia James filed a similar class action suit on behalf of nineteen foster children. She filed the suit against the New York City Administration for Children's Services (ACS) and the New York State Office of Children and Family Services (OCFS) for causing irreparable harm to children in New York City foster care. The public advocate alleges that the agencies failed to protect children from maltreatment or to provide them with permanent homes and families within a reasonable time. One of the plaintiffs had been in foster care for twelve years!

There are foster parents out there doing the best job they can. Most people who work in child services (social workers, administrators, and foster parents) want to do good. But they are working in, and consequently perpetuating, a system that is not aligned with the interests of the people it was built to serve: children.

This, of course, is not lost on the kids.

Pamela Bolnick,[4] who entered foster care at age eight when her schizophrenic mother went off meds, developed a cynical view of her foster parents before completing high school. "All this time, I looked at them as being my own family. I did everything that you'd expect of a child: going to school, not getting into trouble, applying to college," Pamela said. "I came to see it as a business transaction: them being paid [by the government] for taking care of me, and me getting the benefit of being a

---

[3] http://pubadvocate.nyc.gov/foster-care-failures

[4] Pamela Bolnick's story published by NationSwell,
http://nationswell.com/first-place-for-youth-foster-care-transitional-support

child in their custody." Eventually, Pamela ran away from her foster parents.

There is economic incentive to be a foster parent. At the time of this writing, incomes have stagnated or declined for the past several decades. Middle-class life has been slipping out of view for many Americans.[5] So, it's not hard to see the allure of making some extra dollars while ostensibly helping out a needy child (or eight). However, it should go without saying that raising children isn't a "gig" like driving for Uber. Regrettably, this type of monetary incentive can lead to the child warehousing Timothy endured. But there's much more to it than that.

An entire economy has been built around the five hundred thousand children in the American foster-care system. This economy influences federal, state, and local levels of society. It's everywhere around you, hiding in plain sight.

The federal government spends almost $8 billion per year on the Foster Care and Permanency program. That is 15 percent of the $53 billion allotted annually to the Administration for Children and Families, which is the second largest agency in the U.S. Department of Health and Human Services.[6] This kind of money spawns an array of interests vested in perpetuating the system.

In the words of Molly McGrath Tierney, former director of Baltimore's Department of Social Services,[7] "Child welfare is an industry. The only time the federal government pays me is when I take somebody's kid. And as soon as that kid's in foster care they become a commodity. And the industry starts to wrap around: doctors, lawyers, judges, social workers,

---

[5] New York Times, Quantifying the American Dream, http://www.nytimes.com/2016/12/08/opinion/the-american-dream-quantified-at-last.html?_r=0

[6] Administration for Children & Families https://www.acf.hhs.gov/about/budget

[7] Rethinking foster care: Molly McGrath Tierney at TEDxBaltimore 2014 https://www.youtube.com/watch?v=c15hy8dXSps

advocates, whole organizations. The industry is committed to this intervention, this taking other people's children, because that's what it needs to survive."

There's another way to look at this. The foster-care industry is holding half a million American kids hostage. And guess who's paying the ransom?

Chapter Three

One Angry Young Priest

"Hate is not the opposite of love; apathy is."
Rollo May

Fifty years ago, a young priest working in the Massachusetts correction system made an observation: A shocking number of inmates in prison had been in foster care. He was outraged. Not having a family wasn't the fault of the child! Why should an unfortunate turn in a young person's life lead to long-term institutionalization?

Since then, an awful lot has changed: communication, clothes, culture—even the global economy. However, the foster-care-to-prison pipeline hasn't changed. It's the same today as it was in the mid-1960s.

In 1965, Father Paul Engel emerged from almost nine years of cloistered living. He first worked as a Capuchin monk and then as a trainee priest. When he entered the novitiate at age eighteen in 1956, Elvis was climbing up the charts. By the time he was ordained, the British invasion was complete and the world was swinging through a social and sexual revolution. However, Father Paul had neither heard of nor seen any of these changes. He had no access to TV, radio, or newspapers.

The outside world, except the occasional trip home for family emergencies, was unknown to him. While everyone else was dancing the Twist, the Mashed Potato, and the Monkey, he was in bed by 8 p.m. after a day immersed in Latin philosophical texts. His fellow theologians quipped that Latin "first it killed the Romans, now it's killing me."

The Roman Catholic Church was not entirely impervious to change. During Father Paul's final years of sequestering, Vatican II was taking place, an effort initiated by Pope John XXIII to engage with modern society. In November 1964, Father Paul's class was the first to be ordained in the new way, with English in the mass. On rejoining the world, just shy of his twenty-seventh birthday, slender as a whip from ritual penitence and fasting, he felt "so liberated." By June 1965, his studies in theology were complete. He had spent four years in remote Hudson, New Hampshire with the Capuchins then another five in Garrison, New York at the seminary. So, he was delighted to find himself stationed at Our Lady of Sorrows, in Lower Manhattan, his home town.

It was summer in the city, with Lyndon Johnson in the White House and the Great Society in the air. Father Paul started a day camp for kids. His hands on the wheel of a donated bus and God at his side (but without a bus driver's license in his pocket), the young priest created his own "fresh air fund" for the largely Italian and Latin American kids of the parish. That sparked a lifelong interest in helping children. But his halcyon days were numbered. It wasn't long before he found himself relocated to the much smaller Springfield, Massachusetts.

Home to a long tradition of industrial innovation and the headquarters of Smith & Wesson, Springfield's downtown, despite its size, bustled. Crews built highways to connect Western Massachusetts to the national grid, but the roads had not yet sapped vitality from the urban core. Eventually, the highways permanently severed the city from the Connecticut

River, its historic natural artery. St. Francis chapel on Bridge Street, where Father Paul was stationed, served a lively community of lawyers, professionals, and business people. Local residents comprised working-class folks and denizens of nearby single-room occupancy hotels. One such resident was Brian.

Sixteen-years old, Brian worked to support himself and paid $12 per week to live in a hotel room. However, he harbored a very different ambition; he wanted to be a Capuchin friar. Unfortunately, joining a religious order required at minimum a high school diploma. Brian had graduated along a different path, first out of an orphanage and more recently from a reform school for delinquent boys. The school was a cruel, bleak, Dickensian place more attuned to breaking young spirits to instill obedience than to building character and knowledge. When, as a child, his family disintegrated, Brian's life filled with trouble.

Brian and Father Paul crossed paths when the young priest was getting his degree in counseling at nearby Westfield State University. Here was an opportunity to put theory into practice. "And that's where I said, 'let me see what I can do,'" recalls Father Paul. "On the side, I would share his story with people to whom I preached almost every day in the chapel, the people coming to mass. And when the rector wasn't listening, I'd talk about my own requests. One was to find Brian a home. And that's how we connected to Margaret Downey." Margaret, a parishioner at St. Francis, agreed to take Brian under her wing. "It was a moral adoption more than a legal adoption," says Father Paul. "But it was very, very real, right up to her death."

With a home and a mother to guide him, Brian was able to complete his education and become a Capuchin. Today he lives in Guam, still performing religious work. Margaret ultimately took in three other youngsters, in addition to Brian.

Brian's situation was poignant. As part of his studies, Father Paul conducted interviews of inmates at jails in two Western Massachusetts counties, Hampden and Hampshire, where he worked part-time as a chaplain. "Ninety percent in one institution," he remembers, "and almost 98 percent in the other, of those young adults were from foster care." The connection caused a shift in thinking. Rather than merely counsel youth when he completed his degree, Father Paul needed to do something more constructive. He wanted to prevent youngsters like Brian from winding up in jail. The success with Margaret Downey spawned a new idea: Finding wayward youth permanent homes.

In 1967, Father Paul assembled a group of advisors, building its core from the community at St. Francis. Along with Margaret Downey, it included a psychiatrist, Joan Brady, two lawyers, Jim Tourtelotte and Paul Dougherty. This group recruited Father Paul's professor from Westfield, Joe Connelly, with whom he had developed a strong relationship, and the Rev. Mayfield, an Episcopalian minister. The group met at Margaret Downey's house and the new organization took her name. The "Side" in the name provided a counterpoint to a locally renowned orphanage in West Springfield called Brightside. The group was launching an alternative approach, and Downey Side had a ring to it; so, the name stuck.

It's often difficult for people in the twenty-first century to grasp the momentum of social change that swelled throughout the 1960s. Without the Civil Rights Movement and the counterculture riptide that tugged at society from below, today's mainstream population has no real reason to seek alternatives to the status quo. Rapid change today is driven by technology and commerce. We believe the world will be a better place, if we can create the right app.

In Springfield in 1967, this small group of professionals was not part of the counterculture movement, but they were nevertheless swayed by the great tide of deinstitutionalization — or humanizing — running through society at the time. In the field of youth and child development, another British Invasion had been causing waves on this side of the Atlantic.

In the United Kingdom, reform schools such as Finchden Manor, Redfern, St. Francis, and the famous experimental boarding school, Summer Hill, had been championing children's emotional growth, acceptance, care, and openness. This was a radical change from the entrenched, coercive disciplinary model that engendered the same kind of abuses we see in foster care today.

In the book *Last One Over the Wall: The Massachusetts Experiment in Closing Reform School's*, Jerome Miller lists descriptions of documented abuses at the Shirley Industrial School for Boys. He found the evidence in a file of case studies. "Donald, sixteen, beaten on the soles of his bare feet with straps." "Walter, sixteen, handcuffed for twenty-two days and nights when he returned from escape. He was forced to sleep and eat with the handcuffs on." "Charles, seventeen, was padlocked to a water pipe, given a cold shower for six minutes." According to reports in the Boston Globe from that time, "long-term solitary confinement was a regular method of discipline, although it was officially prohibited." (Today, the criminalization of youth, has led to similar practices in jails. It's amazing that certain states are now trying to ban solitary confinement and other psychologically damaging procedures.)

English psychiatrist, Derek Miller, promoted the new British approach in a book that heavily influenced Father Paul. Titled *Growth to Freedom: The Psychosocial Treatment of Delinquent Youth*, Miller's book sought to establish a permanent home for small groups of boys, a place that mimicked a family environment but with psychiatric services. Crucially, the boys' stay in the home would have no termination date; leaving was up to them. Ideally, the home would be located where the youths would like to return after they had matured and gone off into society, just as sons come back to visit their parents after they've moved out and married. The book describes the experimental therapeutic community called Northways, which Miller set up in England in 1961. Two years after leaving Northways, delinquent boys had a recidivism rate of 28 percent compared to 67 percent for a similarly aged control group from traditional institutions.

Downey Side wanted to replicate that experience in Springfield. Paul Dougherty knew the perfect candidate, a young social worker who used to caddy for him at a local country club. Mike Ashe had grown up considerably since the days he chased balls around the back nine for Paul, but the two had stayed in touch while Mike went off to play college football and study history and sociology. Eventually, he finished up with a master's degree in social work from Boston College. After getting married, he moved back to Springfield with a young family while doing clinical work at Holyoke Child Care Center. He later switched to the Division of Child Guardianship, the state-run foster-care program, to work with battered children, the subject of his master's thesis.

Mike loved the work and quickly rose to the level of supervisor. He handled an area of some ninety square miles. But the caseloads were intimidating, up to eighty kids at a time. "You were always putting your finger in the dike, dealing with crisis after crisis and never really having the tools and resources to do well," he said. "But that was the system."

So, when Mike connected with Father Paul and saw his presentation on Downey Side, he understood immediately. "The key aspect it needed was good house parents, good healthy, stable, loving, caring parents. That was the whole thrust of Father Paul's work; needing a family, a permanent family." And, he realized, "It needed leadership."

Mike went home and talked to his wife, Barbara. "I very much identified with the vision because, really, from my standpoint, I'm no longer dealing with crisis after crisis. I go from a caseload of seventy to eighty kids to just dealing with eight kids on a full-time basis. This gives me a wonderful opportunity to really impact kids." Barbara bought in. Mike became Downey Side's first hire.

Mike's professionalism balanced Father Paul's idealism. The priest was aghast when Mike explained just how much money the state was prepared to spend on a child per day, an amount many times higher than Father Paul had guessed. Beyond his understanding of the system, Mike also brought the necessary practical experience of working daily with difficult kids.

They made plans for the agency's first group home. Mike and Barbara were the pilot "House Parents." They would live in the same house with the youth, for all intents and purposes, as a single-family unit—eating together, being involved in every aspect of the boys' lives, giving them a sense of permanency. Fundraising commenced. They solicited donations through various business associations with members connected to St. Francis Chapel. They purchased a handsome three-story Victorian house on Dartmouth Terrace in the central McKnight neighborhood. The agency began the process of getting teenage boys out of institutions and foster homes. They welcomed six youths ages fourteen to seventeen, including two African Americans. Another pair of boys joined a little while later.

Word quickly spread throughout Springfield about Downey Side's work. A recent wave of highly publicized scandals in Massachusetts reform schools had brought to light the maltreatment of their residents. There were "stories of beatings [and] widespread use of solitary confinement, isolation in unheated rooms, rapes, staff discontent, violence, and dilapidated buildings," wrote Jerome Miller, the man who eventually closed them down. (Father Paul was on the committee investigating these deplorable conditions. That committee reported directly to Governor John A. Volpe). The public had a strong appetite for change.

Donations started flooding in. One two-hundred-dollar donation was quickly followed by a call from the donor to Father Paul.

"Is there anything more you need?" asked the woman on the other end.

"Well, I need everything. Beds, chairs ..." replied Father Paul.

"What I want you to do is: Go to this furniture store, and you buy whatever you need for the home and send me the bill," said the donor.

The woman on the line was Connie Breck, of Breck Shampoo, a company famous for its Breck Girl advertising campaigns that ran from the 1930s to the 1980s. The Breck family's support of Downey Side has continued to the present day.

Despite support from influential citizens, a group home for teenagers coming out of correctional institutions was nobody's idea of the perfect neighbor. The NIMBY (Not In My Back Yard) phenomenon was alive near Downey Side decades before it acquired a catchy acronym.

Mike was determined to head off this problem from the outset. "I was very sensitive to those things. I had a lot of confidence that we were going to do the right thing. We wanted to be good neighbors. So immediately after the resistance, when we moved in, we started painting the house." Getting the youngsters involved gave them a sense of investment in their new home. "We would do things to show that we were going to be part of the neighborhood and their property values weren't going to decrease and there wasn't going to be any public safety concerns. If anything, we were going to enhance the neighborhood." Community involvement went deeper than a fresh coat of paint. "We reached out to all the schools. I got the kids involved in the schools. We had after school programs."

Mike was always a real parent to the eight youths who came into his care. "I will say it was very funny. When I look back, here I am this professional social worker, and of course wearing that hat. But you know that the last thing that the kids want is a professional social worker. They want a real father."

So, he did the kinds of things that fathers do. He talked to the boys' teachers. When one of the boys, due to previous sexual abuse, was extremely uncomfortable participating in physical education at high school, Mike persuaded the school to excuse him from gym. This meant the world to the boy. An adult had finally advocated for him, a gesture he remembers to this day.

Because of Mike's deep roots in Springfield, his eyes and ears were everywhere in town. "Everybody knew everybody. We couldn't do jack shit," one of the original house members explains. "He would always find out. Someone would say to Mike. 'Hey, we saw, one of your boys up on Orange Street in a car.' It was uncanny. They were indirectly looking out for us."

Most importantly, Mike's interest in the boys didn't have any "use by" date. Once the boys grew up, he continued to use his connections to find them jobs and give them advice or a temporary home if they needed it. His involvement with the Downey Side boys has remained lifelong, including being a godfather to some of their children.

Daily life at the home resembled a genuine family structure. Everyone ate meals together. Barbara's mother would cook for the whole group. There was no separation between the older non-biological kids and Mike's own family. The boys would read bedtime stories to Mike and Barbara's small children. They visited Mike and Barbara's extended families and took vacations together, once winding up on the Kennedy yacht in Hyannis Port.

This new group home model was a huge improvement on the institutionalized life in reform schools. Encouraged by the progress of Mike's house on Dartmouth Terrace, Downey Side started opening up other homes. The administrators acquired a second place on Liberty Street and placed advertisements in the local papers for additional house parents.

The success of Downey Side got people's attention. A local car dealer, Frank Cantinelli, was particularly impressed. In an astoundingly generous move, he donated the land opposite his Mutual Ford lot on Bay Street to Father Paul, and with it came a house and a barn.

Father Paul moved into the house and set up an office. The relocation made good business sense. The agency had outgrown Margaret Downey's house, but Father Paul still felt his priestly calling. So, he set up an informal chapel in the barn. Before long, Friday night masses with guitar playing and singing drew in many people. Perhaps the barn made the gatherings feel like the original nativity scene. In the late 1960s, "disorganized religion" had far greater appeal to young people than the straight-laced Sunday version.

In addition to helping Father Paul get back to the roots of Christianity, the barn provided a place for the community to mix with the kids from the group homes, an unscripted way to break down barriers. Soon, some members of the community decided to adopt youngsters directly from the group homes.

A seed was planted in the priest's mind.

Chapter Four

Community in Motion

"Our goal is to create a beloved community, and this will require a qualitative change in our souls as well as a quantitative change in our lives."

Dr. Martin Luther King, Jr.

Downey Side took root and spread across Western Massachusetts like a vine. The closing of Massachusetts reform schools in the early 1970s created a favorable environment for community-based initiatives and brought many youngsters to Downey Side's doorstep. At its peak, the agency operated fourteen group homes, as far east as Worcester and as far west as New York border, with two in Pittsfield in the Berkshires. Most clustered around Springfield, West Springfield, Amherst, and Chicopee.

One of the group homes was run by Springfield natives, Elliott and Kay Stratton who unlike Mike Ashe, had no connection to the core group at the St. Francis Chapel. They had discovered Downey Side reading an article in the local paper.

In their early twenties and living in nearby Agawam, they were starting a family and launching professions. Kay was taking time off from teaching to have a baby and Elliott was a substitute science teacher with some additional part-time jobs.

"When I was teaching, you'd see some kid walk in the door and know something was wrong at home," said Elliott. "But how do you help? You just couldn't get close to them. In the classroom there's only fifty minutes a day. How do you help them with the rest of their lives? [As] we discovered [more] about Downey Side, we thought living with them would make a big difference."

"I thought I'd be like Jo in *Little Women*," Kay laughed. "That appealed to me."

After reviewing some files at the Lyman reform school, they interviewed boys as candidates for their home. "We looked at the files first, so we could get an idea," recalled Elliott. "We didn't want to set them up for rejection."

The couple's experience with Downey Side lasted several years in three different houses, always with the same group of boys. They remained committed to the boys for life.

"We helped them through the different stages of development that would naturally happen in a family," said Elliott. "We worked through the natural maturation process. In a regular family it would take eighteen years, but we sort of had to cram it in."

"Some of them didn't even know how to use a phone," explained Kay, "because they'd been institutionalized. But our own kids thought of them as family."

"They called my mother, grandma," Elliott said, recalling a snowed-in Christmas with his extended family.

Their home was a typical Downey Side mishmash of donated items and their own possessions. The group home used a big Pontiac station wagon from a supporter who owned a car dealership. Downey Side also provided a beach house in Westbrook Connecticut for holidays, courtesy of a wealthy donor. The boys saved several boats belonging to neighbors before a storm hit, which helped endear them to the local community, including the teenage girls.

Elliott described the morning meal. "We had a huge kitchen table that came from a bus station. It was a conference room table, and our kids would be there and help prepare the meal."

"Someone told them they couldn't swear in front women, and they didn't," Kay recalled. "The family meal was important. And they would take care of our kids."

As the boys entered high school, Kay and Elliott did all the typical parent-teacher stuff. Bedtime was key too. While tucking the boys in bed, Kay and Elliott listened to them—a new experience for the boys. Because the boys had experienced many difficulties, Kay and Elliott tried to emphasize good things. Bookending their day with personal attention gave them a much-needed sense of continuity. "Like you would with your own kids," noted Kay.

The ad-hoc household was carefully supported by an array of services, including an extensive community of psychiatrists, psychologists and counsellors. The counsellors weren't trained therapists, but the kids could spend time with some people who were a bit closer to their own age. Kay and Elliott's counsellors were conscientious objectors to the Vietnam War doing alternative community service. They also raised funds for Downey Side and performed other roles. These adjunct services helped the house parents as much as the boys.

There were monthly meetings with the house parents. Kay recalled letting some potential house parents know the essential qualities the position required, "You have to be naive, altruistic and a little bit daffy." The work was basically 24/7, despite having two nights off when counsellors would visit to talk to the kids. Elliott said that the support they received helped put all the challenges into perspective.

"They're coming in with a thousand hang-ups. If you can help them with two hundred, you're doing a good job." In retrospect, he said, "We gave them the foundation they never had. It means they were able to have an independent life."

"Tommy had been in twenty-six foster homes and every agency in the state, and he was still looking for his mother down in Florida," Kay said about one of the boys. "His mother took his sister and left him. Talk about rejection."

At times Elliott was forced to physically confront some of the teenagers. Although he never struck any of the kids, one of them hit him. Elliott, with a tremendous amount of self-control, chose not to react. He allowed the teen to use him as an escape valve for his pent-up anger. This unorthodox approach worked, causing the boy to investigate his own feelings.

It's hard to comprehend the blend of fortitude, dedication, and emotional commitment that being a house parent required. Elliott's was a salaried position, but Kay was only paid $12 dollars per week for cooking meals. For them, it was never about the money.

Fully committed for the long-term, Elliott and Kay attended their marriages and helped them raise their own kids. One boy even married Kay's cousin.

Not everything was rosy, of course. Involvement with drugs led one youngster into robbery. He was eventually charged with murder for killing someone during a botched theft. Elliott and Kay helped him throughout the criminal proceedings and continued to visit him in jail after his conviction.

By and large, the placement of "troubled youth" in the community was a success on many levels. The effort removed adolescents from institutionalization, giving them some measure of therapy and a semblance of family life spearheaded by committed adults. The community also got to see that most of the kids, when given the chance, could make their lives work. This success reflected well on Downey Side.

As the home became increasingly known in the area, Mike Ashe called Downey Side a "movement." Springfield became accustomed to local youth raising money in front of supermarkets and at traffic lights.

Downey Side's reputation was also enhanced in unexpected ways. When a group home was to be established in Holyoke, there were objections and a lawsuit as residents feared property values would fall. The suit claimed that the area was only zoned for families, not institutions, with an exception for educational purposes. Downey Side prevailed in court and positive coverage in the local press brought even more adherents into the fold, which proved to be a boon for fundraising.

The group-home model worked well as Massachusetts reform schools emptied; however, the limitations of this approach became increasingly apparent as time passed.

The greatest difficulty was scale. Finding candidates willing to be substitute parents for a large group of troubled youth was (and is) not easy, even with the ancillary support surrounding them. This issue was magnified because the process needed to be replicated over and over. Each group home naturally dissipates as kids reach maturity and move out. After several years of constant involvement with very demanding adolescents, the house parents struggle to take in another group of kids, in part because they remain committed to their original kids even after they've left the nest. The young adults visit and sometimes return, as you'd expect grown family members do. So, the cycle can't be repeated.

About a year after his group home dissolved, Elliott became a juvenile probation officer. In Mike Ashe's case, the maturation of his kids allowed him to pursue another ambition: running for sheriff of Hampden County.

Mike's successful campaign, in 1974, as the first social worker to run for the office in the city's 350-year history is something he credits to Downey Side. "I attribute my success and my election to the grassroots efforts that were taking place in the community out of the Downey Side movement," Mike reflects. "The group homes being creative, being innovative fit sort of a period of anti-institution—a reformation—a new way of looking at things." It's a testament to the reach of Downey Side that Mike was able to win the election.

The job of sheriff in Springfield is not about law enforcement. The assignment involves running the local jails. Mike brought the same spirit of reform that he had applied to his group home. When he built a new jail, he asked all of the deputy sheriffs to spend a night at the new facility in the prisoners' cells—sort like an experiment in customer service—to see for themselves if any improvements could be made.

When I spoke to Mike, he was retiring after serving more than forty years as Sheriff. Among his many achievements, he drastically reduced the number of inmates in his charge and placed them into community-oriented service programs. His successes in that arena are even more extraordinary given that his tenure coincided with America's infatuation with mass incarceration, punitive justice, and prison privatization.

As the 1970s continued, and as several group homes reached their natural maturation as adolescents came of age, Father Paul increasingly questioned the sustainability of the model. By all appearances, the model was thriving and the state was more than content to fund the work. But more and more it felt like a Band-Aid that did not really address the root of the problem.

Father Paul realized that something was fundamentally wrong with the group home structure. In many ways, the group home model was an extension of Margaret Downey's first informal adoption. The group home simply brought more children under one roof. Although group parents were personally dedicated to the kids, they were not their legal guardians.

Father Paul realized that, "The number one principle has to be the protection of the child. I didn't want to do this group home approach anymore. These kids want to be adopted and they must be adopted, and group homes are not sufficient for them."

Even though the group homes de-institutionalized the kids, it seemed simpler to Father Paul to place children directly with families. Many people doubted that families would be willing to adopt adolescents, but he'd witnessed that happen at the barn.

In a radical move, Father Paul decided it was time to close down the group homes. The new model for Downey Side would be to train parents to permanently adopt children. Also, the agency would fill a new role: finding suitable parents. It took a while for this new approach to develop, in part because it required a new legal framework for the agency. And the consequences of shutting down the group homes was immediately apparent. For one, shutting down the group homes also shut off the money.

For Father Paul, this time of change coincided with a feeling of personal crisis. He recalls going through some kind of trauma that lasted many months. "It affected me [while] driving a car, and my eating—it would take me an entire hour to try and digest food. It was just crazy." Today, he refers to it as a sort of "mid-life crisis." Although he doesn't know precisely what triggered the crisis, it's not hard for an outside observer to see why he would struggle. The dissolution of the group homes and the responsibility to develop Downey Side's next phase were daunting challenges

Father Paul took a break from running Downey Side and returned to Garrison, New York. The Downey Side board installed a new director. He was a capable administrator, but he lacked the priest's passion.

Eventually, Father Paul was asked to return to Downey Side as director. Downey side would be reborn as an adoption agency, no longer based in Springfield, but back in New York.

Chapter Five

Inside an Adoption Agency

"There are some things one can only achieve by a deliberate leap in the opposite direction."

Franz Kafka

"Downey Side had to be the first national adoption agency that ever existed in the country," claimed Father Paul. "Because it just didn't exist. All of the agencies grew out of the money schemes in the different states."

The reborn Downey Side began to spread its wings in New York in the early 1980s. There was always some friction between the desires of the state bureaucracy and the aims of the fledgling organization. "What happens with an agency like Downey Side [is that] ACS (Administration of Child Services) wanted to own us. And I said, no," recalled Father Paul. "They want to take you over and require you to only work with them. That's what the government wants because they want that security, and we wouldn't do that."

Downey Side wanted to broaden the pool of children available for adoption. In many ways, adoption is a numbers game. If there are more children for parents to choose from, then the chances of finding a good fit increase. This is especially true when dealing with older children, as Downey Side does. When it's easier to match children with parents, the process moves along faster. That means that less damage is done to the kids. That's the *theory*, anyway. However, as we'll see, rarely does the system move at a pace that is compatible with a child's development.

The first big expansion for the agency was to Minnesota. "There was a group out there that heard about Downey Side," said Father Paul, "and they asked me to come out to speak to them."

Setting up an office far from the East Coast proved to be a major undertaking. The effort gained traction when Brother Terry moved to the state. It still took until 1985 for Minnesota to formalize the license. When that occurred, the agency operated out of two locations, St. Paul and Sauk Rapids. With a foothold firmly established in the Midwest, Downey Side was able to extend its reach, opening an office in Kansas City, Missouri.

"I can only place kids where I'm licensed," explained Father Paul. Just like other professions, adoption agencies must be licensed by the states where they are doing business. Typically, a state's Department of Health and Human Services provides the credentials.

State agencies want to oversee adoption placements because once children are domiciled in their state they are effectively under their watch. For states that are giving up children the reverse is true, the kids are no longer their problem. So, sourcing available children is a different matter, this is facilitated through the Interstate Compact on the Placement of Children (ICPC). Essentially, this "hand-off" means the state of origin is satisfied that the recipient state has done its due diligence.

As Downey Side's reputation grew, more states agreed to place children through the agency. In effect, Downey Side could help kids anywhere in the country find homes in states where it was licensed—in the Midwest and the Northeast. Many of Downey Side's children come from Texas, Maine, Ohio, and even California even though the agency never had an office in these states.

Not everyone in the adoption business needs a license. People such as facilitators and companies that provide online matching aren't strictly vetted by the state because they only perform transactional services. These services often involve sourcing babies from expectant mothers who don't want to keep them. They leave the bulk of the legal work and post-adoptive care up to the adoptive families. Adoption attorneys are, of course, licensed. But they only take care of the legalities. Once the formalities of transferring parental rights have been completed, their job is done. This leaves families to handle the complex emotional and other challenges on their own.

Part of Downey Side's responsibility as a licensed agency is to determine whether a prospective adoptive family can provide an environment conducive to the child's development and safety. This is known as a "home study." It is a very detailed report that is time consuming to produce. It involves extensive background checks—including criminal—and interviews with all family members. The home study constitutes a large portion of the fees charged by most private agencies. (Fees of $15,000 are not unheard of, although Downey Side's fees are on the low end of the spectrum.) In essence, the home study is the foundation upon which all efforts to adopt rest. It's like a family's certificate of worthiness.

As a licensed agency, Downey Side doesn't discriminate against potential adoptive parents, due to ethnicity, race, heritage, or sexual orientation. It also serves single people who are willing to adopt. In the case of potential single parents, home studies can become more complicated; it's trickier to assure the state that sexual partners from outside the home won't pose a risk to children, but this is not an insurmountable issue.

Agencies like Downey Side seek to ensure the continuity of care for the child—or permanence. This doesn't always work out. In some cases, children have been "replaced" with another family due to the inability of the first matched family to adjust and parent a new child or children. Rather than return a child to the foster care system, Downey Side makes every effort to find another adopted home for the children in its care. For this reason, parents go through extensive parent training before the adoption to help them understand the issues children face following the trauma of separation, abuse, neglect, and time in the system. This often entails talking with other Downey Side families who've been through the experience firsthand. It also involves providing all manner of support during and after the placement. States ensure that agencies continue observation for at least another six months.

Finding the right staff is a challenge. Riding the emotional rollercoaster alongside prospective families while simultaneously dealing with the mind-numbing minutia required by child welfare bureaucracies is difficult work. In most states, licensing board consultants perform rigorous background checks and conduct in-person interviews with individuals working for agencies. All for what is best described as a modest salary.

States also scrutinize the financial health of agencies. This is to ensure that agencies won't go out of business and therefore leave adoptive families in the lurch.

I understand all of these requirements, but after many years of involvement, it's hard for me to think of Downey Side as a business. It is a calling. Joy permeates the people in the organization every time a child is placed. I wonder if abolitionists felt this way when they heard about an emancipation.

Downey Side seeks the best interest of children, but children aren't the ones who come knocking on the agency's door. Rather, it's the prospective parents who come. They usually seek help after frustrations with the public system. They are unable to navigate the complexities of the adoption process. Many are losing hope of finding children. That so many make it to the agency after all the discouragement is a testament to their tenacity.

The many Downey Side parents that I've interviewed are driven to adopt. They don't need to be persuaded to add a child to their family. Many have their own birth children. Usually, the mother has the strongest desire and the father plays a supporting role. Among gay couples, very often one partner takes the lead.

I believe that many more prospective families and single parents would adopt if the process weren't so onerous. For this reason, they desperately need guidance. Unfortunately, effective community outreach is difficult for smaller agencies. The demands of running an agency make communications a low priority. Word-of-mouth "marketing," as is evident in Downey Side's case, has been the most reliable source of referrals. But that approach also means that the agency will have a narrower sphere of influence.

I teamed up with a communications company to rebrand Downey Side and built a new website. Everyone enjoyed working on a project that clearly had a positive social impact. In fact, the board of the communications company had to pull its CEO aside and tell her to ease up on the Downey Side project. The company had been donating so much labor that it was impacting the bottom line. The cause of finding permanent families for children inspires regular people.

However, there aren't that many families who want to adopt children. That's understandable because agencies like Downey Side lack resources to help prospective parents. How many prospective parents give up along the arduous journey, exhausted and frustrated by the ordeal? If more could make it through, far fewer kids would be in foster care.

This points to one of the crucial failings of our current system: There is a complete misalignment of resources. Father Paul will tell you that the biggest difference between the original group-home model and the adoption agency is the state's willingness to pay. And of course, in the original model, the state remains the child's legal guardian.

Chapter Six

Trying to Adopt: Hostage Negotiations

"If you live your life as a hostage to everybody else's decision, you either have to live a very narrow life, or you have to spend a lot of time in pain."

Newt Gingrich

How hard is it to adopt children from foster care?

Imagine a hostage situation. Someone is armed and barricaded in room with a group of victims. It's all very intense and traumatic. A skillful negotiator shows up, diffuses the tension, and it's over in a matter of hours. If you think foster care is like this, think again. Getting children out of foster care is akin the Iran Hostage Crisis in 1980, which took 444 days to get fifty-two Americans freed from Tehran. In fact, it often takes much longer.

One Downey Side family came to the agency for help after a five-year odyssey to adopt children from foster care. We'll call them the Cliffs because they've been on the precipice so often. To describe their journey as an emotional rollercoaster doesn't do justice to their perseverance; after all, a rollercoaster ride only lasts a couple of minutes.

In April 2018, the Cliffs were finally able to adopt two adorable brothers. But over a five-year period, they had to endure three failed attempts to adopt children from Florida, Michigan, and California. Each failure came at tremendous emotional cost to both them and the children they hoped would join their family.

Although each family's experience is unique, the Cliffs' painful experiences illustrate a clear pattern in the difficulty of getting kids out of the system. Their story is described in the pages that follow.

The Cliffs, who live in New Jersey, considered international adoption after failing to get anywhere in their home state's system. However, Mrs. Cliff ultimately decided to adopt domestically. "With international adoption there was no matching," she said. "It's just like, 'oh, here, take this child regardless' and, at least in theory, in the US foster-care system, they want to match the children with the family that can take care of their specific needs and is compatible in other ways. And we thought that was a good thing."

New Jersey's foster-care system has two parallel tracks for would-be adoptive parents. You can either adopt *within* the state through the government system, or you can adopt from *out of state* with the help of a private agency. The state system is free. Private agencies, including Downey Side, can charge fees that range very widely.

One of the fundamental flaws of the US foster-care system is the immense degree of fragmentation across the country. Each state has its own approach to adoption. This compounds the bureaucracy and increases the burdens for families wanting to adopt. The Cliff's opted to adopt out of state for several reasons. First, they had tried and failed in New Jersey before. Second, they knew others, including a neighbor, who had given up on the state and went private. Finally, they believed their "chances of getting matched with children would be a lot greater if we had the whole country to choose from and not just little New Jersey." They were playing a numbers game.

Potential adoptive parents must first apply to the state. Like almost everything to do with child welfare, this varies from state to state. The goal is to provide basic information—family composition, the number of people in the home—as well as enabling background checks on any household resident over 18 years old to determine if they have abused a child or a have a criminal record. Potential parents also give the state a run-down on the type of child they are seeking. The idea is to ensure children are placed with families best suited to the child's needs.

Next comes the home study, which is an in-depth process that attempts to create a three-dimensional portrait of the adoptive family. Meetings, interviews, and training sessions help agencies (both private and state-run) decide whether a family is ready to adopt. It's an intense experience in which a family is subjected to a lot of scrutiny. Many families withdraw at this stage. After several months, this investigation concludes when the agency's case worker produces a written report, which the family gets to review. Once the home study is approved by the state, it becomes the blueprint for matching children in foster care with the potential family.

The cost of doing a home study ranges considerably. It can be free, when performed by a state agency, or cost up to $15,000 depending on the private agency. There could be additional expenses, such as paying for fingerprints. This fee is paid without any guarantee that a child will be placed.

The Cliffs used the private approach because they wanted access to a wider pool of children. Even though the state pathway would provide a free home study, Mrs. Cliff didn't fancy her chances. "[Going through the state] is much harder because you don't have anybody to advocate for you. The state advocates for the children, which is right, but if you don't have anybody to advocate for you—and there's always competition—it's very unlikely that you're going to end up adopting."

Although the Cliff's had a home study done in 2010 when they lived in Florida, they needed a new one when they moved back to New Jersey several years later. This is one of the many catch-22 situations that parents face when trying to get kids out of foster care. States will recognize each other's home studies during interstate adoptions; however, if potential parents move to another state, their home study becomes invalid. There is no national standard. So, the Cliffs redid it in New Jersey and began looking for children. This led to two very close opportunities to place children in their home. But both times their hopes were dashed.

In December of 2016, a group of four siblings (two boys and two girls) captured the Cliffs' hearts. "I found these children on California Kids Connection, the state listing for California," Mrs. Cliff recounted, adding that the process was similar to online dating. "They have a picture and a description of the child, and then you submit a form, and their form allows you to make comments." Like a lot of kids in foster care, the four children came from an abusive family.

According to Mrs. Cliff, the children's father had severely abused them. He was put in jail for physical and sexual abuse. He had so neglected them that they never went to school. The father singled out the oldest son for cruel torment, breaking his arm so many times it is permanently deformed. At one point, the boy was taken away from the family for a year. However, he returned to the terrible situation for another seven years. As a result, this child was extremely aggressive. He took his anger out on his younger brother.

Because of this behavior, the Cliff's thought the oldest boy was more than they were equipped to handle. When they expressed their reservations to their adoption worker, Mrs. Cliff expected the state to tell them goodbye. To her surprise, they didn't. "They said, 'if you will take the other three children, you can do it—as long as you keep in contact with the fourth child.' We said, 'Fine. We'll do it.'"

This happy moment initiated months of living on a razor's edge. Even though the Cliffs had been matched with their prospective adoptive children, it was no guarantee that the placement would go through. In fact, that's when the emotional rollercoaster starts clanking up the first incline. Having ridden it twice before, in Michigan and Florida, the coupled steeled themselves. "My husband was like, 'I can't believe we're really adopting these children because we believed in the past and it just didn't work out. So, you have to protect yourself,'" said Mrs. Cliff.

California has its own processes. The most vexing, from the adoptive parent's point of view, is that the state will not terminate the parental rights (known as TPR) of the birth parents until a prospective adoptive match is in place. This ostensibly prevents the state from creating "orphans" and keeps the government out of the business of parenting—a laudable goal. However, the children are still in foster care, regardless. Thus, the state regulation creates an agonizing situation in which abusive birth parents get the chance to redeem themselves before a judge and, in essence, contest the adoption.

To add fuel to this legal inferno, California requires those involved to explore the possibility of placing children with relatives and friends. So, once suitable adoptive parents have been identified, the system triggers a new set of legal procedures that leave children in foster-care limbo. The lumbering tempo of an overly clogged court system fails to keep up with the lightning pace of a child's development.

In January, the Cliffs got word that relatives of the children were interested adopting them. It seemed likely that would happen. Despondent, the couple wondered if they should start looking again. Then, in March, they discovered to their delight that the relatives were deemed unsuitable. The Cliffs had been officially matched with the children. California would terminate the birth parents' parental rights and schedule a hearing in May.

At this point, the Cliffs were encouraged to have contact with the children. The couple began in April to call them twice a week, which amounted to four calls a week because the girls and the boys were in separate foster homes. When the Cliffs attended a wedding in California, they were able to meet the children in person and spend time with them over the course of a month out West. A bond developed.

However, when the hearing was convened in May, the relatives reappeared. They claimed to have solved whatever issues had previously prevented them from taking charge of the children. The judge duly ruled that the social workers needed to keep the option of sending the children to the relatives open.

Communication between the Cliffs and the children halted.

This time, the social workers were able to rule out the relatives in a mere two days. Apparently, whatever changes the relatives had made were either insufficient or cosmetic.

When the Cliffs were able to contact the children again, the children were anxious. One of the girls wanted to know why the Cliffs hadn't called. Sadly, explaining the workings of the California legal system to an eight-year old was beyond Mrs. Cliff's abilities.

Although communication resumed, uncertainty did not abate. The judge set the next TPR hearing for the end of July. Even though the social workers had reached a swift conclusion, the endless waiting continued at the glacial rate of the court.

The Cliffs thought about implementing a few strategies to accelerate this lethargic process. First, they could move to California. Given the flexible nature of their jobs and because they had extended family in the area, this was possible. Living in California would enable them to serve as the foster family for the children, which under California law supposedly makes it easier to adopt the kids in your care. But a move would force the Cliffs to do another home study in California, which takes six to nine months and another round of expenses.

They also toyed with the notion of fostering the kids in New Jersey and then adopting them. However, according to Mrs. Cliff, California shot down the idea of moving the children to another state. They couldn't serve as the children's foster parents in a different state because the state is only allowed to pay foster parents who live in California. The couple offered to foster the kids without the money. The response was an unequivocal no.

At the end of July, the court was too overwhelmed to deal with the case. The hearing was postponed for yet another month.

In the meantime, the birth mother had turned to social media to solicit new relatives to lay claim to the children. Now the court would have to officially rule out the previous relatives, whom the social workers had already deemed unfit, and they would have to evaluate two new relatives and a family friend who showed interest in adopting the children.

Word from the social worker in California was discouraging. She felt that California typically favors friends and relatives in these situations, and that the state was leaning toward the family friend. The Cliffs were heartbroken. It looked like they would be unmatched, yet again.

Despite this, the Cliffs were advised to continue talking to the children. One of children had a birthday, so the Cliffs sent gifts (with her social worker's approval). The Cliffs were looking for a new dog and one of the girls asked if she could name it.

This tenuous, painful situation continued. The birth mother was set to appeal whatever decision was made. Everyone was walking a tightrope.

Especially the children.

The Cliffs questioned the wisdom of keeping the two brothers together in foster care in close quarters. They sympathized with the foster parents who had to keep a constant eye on the older boy due to his abusive actions against his younger sibling. However, it seemed that the boys' foster parents had been doing a better job of preparing them for adoption than the family looking after the two sisters.

The girls had moved to a second foster home after a year. Then it became difficult for the Cliffs to stay in touch with them. Even though they always called the girls at the scheduled time, they often got no answer. When calls did go through, they often weren't able to talk to the younger girl because she was being punished, taking a nap, doing yard work, or eating dinner.

When the Cliffs visited the children in California, they could see a stark contrast between the two foster homes. "The little boy, he was all dressed up in new Sunday best clothes, which his foster mother said he wanted to do," said Mrs. Cliff. "It was obvious that she had been talking to him about us and he was excited and happy." At the girls' home, the Cliffs received a completely different welcome. The older girl was afraid. When asked if she could be hugged, she said no. Instead, she allowed Mrs. Cliff to hug her doll. It took nearly all day for the child to warm up to her prospective parents.

As for the little boy, the Cliffs had been able to share family videos with him, which was easy to do iPhone-to-iPhone with the foster mother's help. But with the girls, they had to adhere to strictly regimented landline calls. To overcome this frustration, they brought two cheap tablet devices with them on their visit. As Mrs. Cliff explained, "We were told we were supposed to be Skyping with the children twice a week, but we haven't been able to do that because we have to talk to them on the landline. We can't send them pictures." The social worker told them she couldn't force the foster parents to do anything. But Mrs. Cliff found it hard to believe that no one in the house had a cell phone. In the end, she said, "We didn't give the devices to them and we didn't give them to the boys either because we didn't want to cause competition or jealousy. So, we just brought them back from California."

A greater concern was that the littlest girl, who was turning nine, could not read at all. Mrs. Cliff, a trained English teacher, despaired. "If she were in my house, I'd be tutoring her in reading. But she's not in my house. She's somewhere in California where they're just fooling around all summer." Moreover, the girl had to go to two schools in one year because she had been forced to switch foster homes. All of this meant she would enter third grade not knowing how to read.

According to Mrs. Cliff, the boys also started out with poor literacy, but they had been able to catch up. She attributed their progress to a more attentive foster family and therapy. The girls, who lived an hour and a half away, had neither.

The conditions of foster care exacerbate the emotional tightrope walk. "We were acutely aware of how they were being hurt by being stuck in the system," lamented Mrs. Cliff. "Some of them were very behind in school and had medical needs, but those needs were not being addressed. We felt so frustrated that we were not able to do anything about those things because we had no legal status."

This long-term uncertainty stretched the essential bond between the potential adoptive family and the children. If an adoption doesn't go through, contact is usually lost forever. Here's how Mrs. Cliff described the experience, in an email.

We were attached to them and cared what happened. We knew, however, from previous experiences that if we lost the match, we would not even be told what happened to them. We had a previous match that did not work out in which the nasty judge told me and ruled in open court that we were not allowed to know what would happen to the children. This was after they had been placed with us, but we were not able to keep two of them due to their unsafe behavior. They were literally ripped from our arms in tears. It's a bad business!

Fortunately, that was not the case this time.

At the hearing in August, the judge decided in favor of the Cliffs. The judge dismissed the other petitions and terminated the parental rights of the birth parents.

Even so, the Cliffs were still not in the clear. The birth parents appealed the decision. According to the Cliff's social worker, California typically judges appeals on procedural mistakes rather than by the merits of the case. So, the Cliffs remained guardedly optimistic that the appeal would also be dismissed.

Having finally jumped through this exhausting and drawn-out legal hoop, the Cliffs had to steel themselves for the next ordeal: the Interstate Compact on the Placement of Children, generally known as the ICPC.

The ICPC was originally drafted fifty-nine-years ago to ensure the safety and stability of placements across state lines. But as the government's own website[8] says, "the 1960 ICPC has not kept pace with major changes in child welfare practice and technology, and placement across state lines can still present difficulties and delays." This is something of an understatement.

[8] Child Welfare Information Gateway
https://www.childwelfare.gov/topics/permanency/interjurisdictional/icpc/

The speed with which individual states can process ICPC paperwork varies enormously. The Cliffs had been told to expect California's process to take between ninety and 120 days, meaning a year after they had first encountered the children online.

"The whole ICPC thing is a stupid game in my opinion, totally unnecessary," said Mrs. Cliff. "Why does what state we live in matter?"

Meanwhile, the eldest sibling had been placed with a family in California just days after the TPR hearing. Knowing this frustrated the Cliffs. "We had a valid home study and were chosen for the children just like the other family," Mrs. Cliff said.

With all the advances of the past six decades, it's hard to believe that it should take so long for one state to verify work already completed by another state. Processing information today is lightyears faster. Our twenty-first century economy is built on it. Why has the country done nothing to speed up the process to connect permanent families to the nation's most vulnerable children? What does that say about our priorities?

Flowchart is a misnomer for a process that does anything but flow. The figure overleaf is really a map of bottlenecks. When looking at the diagram, it's evident that much of the ICPC process is one state duplicating the paperwork of another.

A big question regarding the whole process remains: Is this in the best interests of the child?

Which takes us back to the hostage issue.

Taking a child from the family obviously damages the child. But the longer the child is in a state of limbo, unable to attach to a new family, the worse they fare. The cruelty of perpetuating such suffering through needless bureaucracy is inhumane to everyone: the parents, the social workers, and especially the children.

Who benefits from this? The only winner is system.

FLOWCHART OF THE ICPC PROCESS

SENDING AGENCY Agency where child resides	• Completes ICPC form 100-A. • Requests home study, including outline of local requirements. • Sends information packet about child's special needs, proposed medical and financial arrangements to support the placement, and necessary services for the child. **1**	• If receiving state approves placement, reviews home study and other information to determine whether to place child out of state. • If child is to be placed in receiving state, completes ICPC Form 100-B. • Notifies receiving state that the child has been placed and supervision by that state is to begin. • Retains financial responsibility and court jurisdiction for case. **7**	• Uses progress reports to assess ongoing placement. • Considers and recommendations received. • If needed, continues to consider permanency plans for the child (including finalization of cross jurisdictional adoption). **13**

SENDING STATE ICPC Compact Administrator in child's state	• Reviews packet for completeness and compliance with state laws. • Forwards packet to receving state. **2**	• Reviews home study for completeness and compliance with state laws. **6**	• Reviews ICPC Form 100-B. **8**	• Monitors periodic progress reports. • Reviews any recommendations. **12**

RECEIVING STATE ICPC Compact Administrator in prospective guardian's state	• Reviews packet for completeness and compliance with state laws. • Asks receiving agency to review proposed placement **3**	• Reviews home study for completeness and compliance with state laws. • Upon reveiwing recommendations, approves or denies requested placement. • Signs ICPC form 100-A. **5**	• Reviews ICPC Form 100-B. **9**	• Monitors periodic progress reports. • Reviews any recommendations. **11**

RECEIVING AGENCY Agency where prospective guardian resides	• Conducts home study. • Makes recommendation about the suitability of potential placement **4**	• Conducts supervision of child's case. • Ensures that requested services are received. • Prepares periodic progress reports. • If appropriate, recommends closing case or returning child to the sending state. **10**

Adapted from the GAO's November 1999 – HHS Could Better Facilitate the Interjurisdictional Adoption Process
The Pennsylvania Child Welfare Resource Center

Chapter Seven

The Belly of the Beast

Hell isn't merely paved with good intentions; it's walled and roofed with them. Yes, and furnished too.

Aldous Huxley

What is foster care supposed to do? The simple answer: protect children.

The government protects children in a basic manner, by intervening and getting kids out of harm's way. But at what price? A growing body of child welfare specialists have joined the chorus calling for the end of foster care as the default solution for troubled families. Many realize how harmful it is to separate children from parents, even for short periods.

The most significant step toward eliminating foster care is to stop children from entering it in the first place. If we can stop children going into foster care and focus on getting the remaining ones out of the system as fast as possible, then the number of children in the system will shrink to zero.

Physical abuse accounts for only 12 percent[9] of child removals.

[9] https://www.acf.hhs.gov/cb/resource/afcars-report-24

Neglect is by far the most common reason for children entering foster care. According to the Children's Bureau, neglect is evident in 61 percent[10] of all cases.

What is neglect?[11] It's defined as the failure of a parent, guardian, or other caregiver to provide for a child's basic needs. These include things such as food, shelter, medical care, education, and attention to the child's emotional wellbeing. In 34 percent of the cases, neglect results from parental drug abuse (the bureau's fourteen categories are not mutually exclusive). With the opioid epidemic sweeping the nation, the number of children suffering drug-induced neglect is on the rise.

Neglect shows up in both the child's and parent's behavior in predictable and recognizable ways. Many of these appear when a child is at school.

Signs of neglect in children are apparent in the following ways:

• Sudden changes in behavior or school performance
• Lack of medical help for physical problems
• Learning and attention difficulties that aren't attributable to physical or psychological causes
• Being perpetually on guard, expecting something bad to happen
• Becoming withdrawn, overly compliant, or passive
• Coming to school or other activities early, staying late, and not wanting to go home
• Showing reluctance to be around a particular person
• Disclosing maltreatment

Parents, too, give signals that they are mistreating their kids:

[10] https://www.acf.hhs.gov/cb/resource/afcars-report-24
[11] https://www.childwelfare.gov/pubs/factsheets/whatiscan

- Denying the existence of—or blaming the child for—the child's problems in school or at home
- Asking teachers or other caregivers to use harsh physical discipline if the child misbehaves
- Viewing the child as entirely bad, worthless, or burdensome
- Demanding a level of physical or academic performance the child cannot achieve
- Wanting the child to satisfy the parent's emotional needs instead of the parent satisfying the child's
- Showing little concern for the child

The interactions between children and parents also yield clues. These include poor eye contact, lack of healthy affection, negative talk about the other person, or stating they don't like each other.

The line between poverty and neglect is often blurred. Is a child left alone because the parent can't afford child care? Are they missing meals because there isn't enough money to feed or clothe them? Does the child miss doctor appointments because the parent is fearful that taking time off from work might lead to unemployment?

Brother Terry Taffe, a Capuchin friar and social worker who was part of Downey Side for many years before setting up his own organization in one of New York's poorest neighborhoods, put it this way.

Families lose their kids, for the most part, to neglect. They're not losing their kids to abuse. The neglect is like being $500 short each month. That's a big amount of money if you don't have it. You're just screwed in New York City. It's the choice between an apartment or food.

In New York, kids are going to come to the attention

of authorities. There is phenomenal psychological pressure when you take that money away. Penury creates physical and psychological hardships that make it nearly impossible to get that kid to school on time, to get that kid in school dressed in clean clothes, with food. So, the school says, 'There's something going on here. Oh my God,' and calls up the city. [The city] says, 'I'm not sure if you're abusing the kid or just neglecting the kid, and I'm not sure that you're a good parent. I'll tell you what, let's cut a deal: Put the kid in [our] care and we will work on your issues.'

State and city agencies react when neglect is brought to their attention. Some type of intervention is clearly necessary. "It's not just poverty, it's not just a physical thing. You've got drugs and alcohol, you've got internal violence, and all those issues that come along with poverty," elaborated Brother Terry,

But should the first reaction be to remove the child? Shouldn't that be the very last course of action?

Neglect itself is a symptom, the product of multiple stresses occurring simultaneously in a family. Most people want to be good parents. Some don't know how. And many don't have the resources to manage the responsibilities of parenting.

The real challenge is to detect neglect early and then to relieve the stress by supporting the family before a crisis develops. The $500 that some parents need is another $3.13 per hour for someone working forty hours per week. In the eighteen states where minimum wages have been pegged to cost-of-living increases, there is hope that some hardship will be reduced.

Family impoverishment is clearly a huge risk factor for children entering foster care. It's a truism that middle-class children do not end up in the system. Money doesn't *solve* everything, but it is *part of* everything in our society. For the sake of children stuck in the nation's foster-care system, deciding how we direct spending deserves the utmost scrutiny.

Each year the federal government spends approximately $4.3 billion on foster care. By comparison, only $652 million[12] goes to prevention and permanency services. That means that for every dollar spent on prevention, almost seven are spent on a broken system.

Where does this money go?

As of this writing, New York State pays foster parents $535 ($586 in metropolitan New York) monthly per child age five and under. For those twelve and older, New York pays $746 ($802 in metropolitan New York). For "special children," payment swells to $1289, and for "exceptional children"[13] the payment is $1953. (The term special children includes those with physical issues, delinquency, or diagnosed moderate developmental or emotional difficulties. Exceptional children, require some form of twenty-four-hour care or have been diagnosed with severe emotional and behavioral issues.) Additional allowances and payments exist for clothing, diapers, and sundry needs.

If Brother Terry's anecdotal observation is accurate, then supporting existing families is in many ways a better return on our social investment, or at least a cost-neutral solution.

This type of monthly support for foster parents is only part of the picture. The vast pools of money spent on foster care are siphoned off throughout the system. The trauma caused in children by separating them from parents creates psychological and medical conditions that require attention. So, in addition

[12] Casey Family Programs report based on Child Maltreatment 2015 and 2015 data made available by the National Data Archive on Child Abuse and Neglect (NDACAN), including the Adoption and Foster Care Analysis and Reporting System (AFCARS) and the National Child Abuse and Neglect Data System (NCANDS)

[13] https://ocfs.ny.gov/main/rates/fostercare/rates/FC-Board-2016Jul01-2017Mar31.pdf

to any existing problems a child may have due to neglect, they are now launched into a feedback loop of new issues caused by family separation and frequent rotations through different homes. A view into any foster child's case file will reveal that they often require medical and psychological evaluations, all at the expense of the state.

The system's tentacles wrap around every part of a child's existence. Doctors, psychologists, lawyers, social workers, and advocates in the foster care industrial complex must all be paid. These individuals no doubt embark on a career in child services hoping to help, but in the end, they become subordinate to the system and its self-perpetuation. With half a million kids in the system, it's easy to see how the cost starts to rack up.

People may imagine that foster care is like a giant dispersed orphanage: lots and lots of kids in many thousands of homes waiting for new parents to adopt them. In reality, the foster-care system is mostly used as a massive holding pen for children whose parents are in the process of sorting out their lives—at the direction of the government.

Of the nearly five hundred thousand children in foster care, the stated goal of the federal Children's Bureau for more than half (55 percent)[14] is for the children to return to their parents or principal caregivers, usually after they've received some sort of treatment and/or training. The system is focused mostly on intervening between neglectful parents and their kids. That means that nearly 275,000 times per year children are separated from the family. There is no doubt that breaking the parent-child bond is one of the most detrimental things you can do to a child. Yet that is our answer.

The government's objective has come under scrutiny from a

---

[14] https://www.acf.hhs.gov/sites/default/files/cb/afcarsreport24.pdf

variety of sources, including the media. On July 17, 2017, *The New York Times* ran a blistering story titled "Foster Care as Punishment: The New Reality of 'Jane Crow.'"[15] The article detailed scenarios in which children had been taken from their parents for what the newspaper described as mere "hiccup(s) in the long trial of raising a child." The writer quoted Scott Hechinger, a lawyer at Brooklyn Defender Services.

There's this judgment that these mothers don't have the ability to make decisions about their kids, and in that, society both infantilizes them and holds them to superhuman standards. In another community, your kid's found outside looking for you because you're in the bathtub, it's 'Oh, my God'—a story to tell later. In a poor community, it's called endangering the welfare of your child.

The New York Times story was provoked by a sudden spike in the number of New York City's parent-children separations, in the first few months of 2017. Because child welfare is not on the general public's radar, the issue only gets attention when something makes headlines. Usually, this is some horrific event, such as the murder of Zymere Perkins, a six-year-old boy beaten to death with a broken broomstick by his mother's boyfriend in Harlem. Shortly after Zymere's death, three-year-old Jaden Jordan died after his mother's boyfriend assaulted him. The ensuing media furor led Gladys Carrion to resign. She was the head of the Administration of Child Services and a respected advocate for children. The media storm also caused a 40 percent increase of children entering foster care in the city.

---

[15] https://www.nytimes.com/2017/07/21/nyregion/foster-care-nyc-jane-crow.html

Molly McGrath Tierney, former head of Baltimore's Social Services department in her TEDx[16] talk, called systemic parent-child separation an "oppression" that many poor people see as a coercive weapon.

Gerald (Garry) Mallon, an associate dean and professor of child welfare at Hunter College's Silberman School of Social Work in New York believes that frequent leadership turnover within child welfare services is common nationwide. The intermittent press scrutiny following a newsworthy failure keeps executives in fight-or-flight mode, and that inhibits changes to the system. Everyone wants to cover their ass.

Our current approach punishes poor parents and asks social workers to predict the future, to assess the likelihood that poverty will lead to neglect and neglect to abuse. While humans are mentally equipped to see patterns in past events, we're notoriously inept at prognostication. Why should we expect social workers to predict the future better than the rest of us? One critic, writing about the Zymere Perkins case, said that the social workers were guilty of not being able read minds.

Given the dire consequences of a judgment error, it's easy to see why the "safest route" is to remove the child; "safe," that is, in regard to saving one's own job and saving the department from embarrassment. However, the system is not safe for the long-term prospects of the child.

The political and professional consequences of mistakes are too high to make real change, so we end up with the wrong type of reform. All we do is tinker with the system's efficiency. We cause harsher enforcement for increasingly trivial indiscretions leading to the separation of more children from parents. The system isn't designed to help children or families. It exists to perpetuate itself.

[16] https://www.youtube.com/watch?v=c15hy8dXSps

At least something is being done when children are at risk of dying. But that's a fool's choice. We shouldn't have to choose between a child beaten to death or thousands of children suffering the effects of forced parent-child separations. It's important to remember that the system's short-term fixes have lifelong consequences for children.

The foster care system is full of well-intended folks determined to save children. Child welfare is not something that attracts fortune hunters. We shouldn't point fingers at social workers, the foot soldiers of child welfare. They observe at-risk families, admit kids into the system, monitor them, argue in court, oversee each transfer to a new foster home, and evaluate the fitness of adoptive parents.

However, the reams of paperwork social workers produce is the grease that lubricates the system. A single case file of information on a child—physical, mental, legal evaluations—can quickly grow to be inches thick. Dealing with case files can become the focus of their labor, not the child. Ironically, sometimes social workers' emotions get the best of them; they form attachments to children, which can actually hinder the child's progress through the system.

Social workers employed by state and non-state agencies, not surprisingly, have their own perspectives on foster care. But it's hard to find any who have enthusiasm for the system's current condition. In many places, the caseloads are overwhelming, burnout is high, and the workers' sense of purpose is diminished to ash. That's a lot to ask from workers who often need a master's degree and whose average salary is $49,500[17] nationally.

"The people working in child welfare want to have more impact," Tierney asserts. "If they were presented with a different way, people would jump at the chance."

[17] glassdoor.com

A different way would require us as a nation to shift our focus and our resources to prevention rather than intervention, to supporting families instead of being punitive. Changing government policies that have developed over decades, molded institutional thinking, and created an industry is not going to be easy.

But it is possible. We should listen to social workers about what does work. Leora Neal, who ran the New York Chapter of the Association of Black Social Workers Child Adoption and Counseling and Referral Service for over two decades, thinks the attitude adjustment begins with simple steps. "Instead of trying to find something wrong, let's catch people doing something right! People always tell you when you're doing wrong but they never tell you when you're doing right." As any behavioral scientist will tell you, encouragement, also known as positive reinforcement, goes a long way.

What does positive reinforcement look like in practice? Let's say a parental neglect case is brought to the attention of authorities. Neal says that social workers can go to the family and say, "How can I help?" rather than going to them as an investigator. She participated in an alternative program in which birth parents' typical antipathy toward social workers was turned around. "They started looking forward to their worker coming and served cups of tea and cookies." That's a far cry from the "Jane Crow" depicted in the Times.

Many parents, Neal maintains, simply lack basic knowledge about child development. For example, "not knowing what it's like to deal with two-year olds," she said. "A lot of children come into care because of what do they do at two. They start saying 'no' all the time and if you don't understand that it's just a developmental stage, that they say 'no' even when they mean yes, then you can get angry." With all the other stresses occurring due to poverty, it doesn't take much for that anger to turn to neglect and fester into abuse.

Foster kids eventually grow up and become adults. Sadly, Neal witnesses an ongoing cycle in which gaps in knowledge get perpetuated over generations.

A lot of kids come out of foster care and they haven't learned how to parent and so their kids go back into foster care. They've been bounced around so much, and people don't understand the detriment that happens. You can't just pick up and move, it traumatizes them, it's more than just a move. They have to adjust to a whole new way of thinking and family life. So, what was acceptable in one family is not acceptable in another. There's no consistency. And that's why their brain is going 'bing, bing, bing' and why they develop a coping mechanism that shuts down a lot. They change neighborhoods, they change schools, they change religions, they change expectations, and so on. Who are you really? They don't know. And a lot of kids nowadays just get medicated when they start showing problems.

All the things that people should learn outside of school about how to be in a family, the skills needed to successfully start one of your own, are missing or badly jumbled among people who were raised in foster care.

Even when kids do get adopted, they face another hurdle when seeking treatment for the emotional damage. According to Neal, "Adoptive parents always talk about the difficulty in finding therapists who really understand children who have had more than one set of parents." It's not an area covered in psychological training. Growing up with one set of two parents is complicated enough, as anyone who's been in therapy can testify. Foster care multiplies and multiplies the psychological complexities.

In light of all this damage to children, are we really protecting them?

There are two common political responses to the system's problems. The typical conservative approach is to cut funding for child services. The classic liberal reaction is to throw more money at it. But neither approach will matter if we don't fundamentally alter the mission. Right now, we intervene too late and too harshly. Then we spend too long trying to patch up broken families. All this damages children as they cycle endlessly through the foster-care system.

What would it look like if we spent seven times more money on supporting families and finding permanent homes for kids than we do on foster care? If we did that, we'll likely discover that we don't need foster care at all.

Chapter Eight

Some Solutions

"A correct answer is like an affectionate kiss."

Johann Wolfgang von Goethe

Preventing kids from entering foster care and speeding up the adoption process will shrink the number of children in foster care. If these processes happened quickly enough, we'd close in on the desired goal of having zero children languishing in the system. To this end, we'll look at some existing solutions that are currently working, and some possible solutions that could be implemented.

Many kids in foster care eventually wind up in the care of family members who are not their biological parents. The name for this is "kinship adoption." It has been practiced informally throughout human history. According to Leora Neal, children who live with their aunts, uncles, or grandparents aren't subject to the same kind of stigma that foster kids experience. And the familiarity of being with relatives often means separation and bonding problems aren't as pronounced.

Surely there are ways to expedite this. One suggestion, from Father Paul, is to establish a chain of custody for children prior to their births. Just as godparents serve as moral guardians in

Christian families, the people in the chain of custody would commit to adopt the child should the need arise.

If such a legal framework existed, and if the chain of custody could be documented with the child's birth certificate, then much of the court's work would already be done. Naturally, this would require expecting parents to carefully consider who is suitable, willing, and able to fill the role. Subsequently, during childhood, the parents would have to periodically reevaluate their designations as the circumstances of the stand-in parents change.

This idea points to a larger problem in society, particularly for those at the margins: the general lack of parenting knowledge and skills. (Leora Neal mentioned this problem in an earlier chapter.) Clearly, if we want to reduce the number of kids entering foster care, we need to make parenting education available to anyone who needs it.

Supporting families in need is an issue that social worker Anita Alvarez spoke about at length with me. Alvarez is an early childhood teacher who works with young mothers and children in the Bronx in New York.

"When a parent brings in a child, we should check on the parent, too," she said. "It's the perfect time to assess if the home environment is not right and what's needed to help parents keep it together." Parents, she said, need more support. "Not just money. They need to learn how to budget. When you ask questions at intake, it's surprising how honest the answers are. People want to be good parents. But kids don't come with instructions."

At the center where Alvarez works, she estimates that 99 percent of the population live in the city's homeless shelter system. They're often there for three-to-five years. As she has navigated the complexities of the welfare system, she has seen how its onerous work obligations affect mothers. However, she has also observed a significant benefit from the city's recently implemented universal, free pre-K program. If parents can enroll their children in school, they are freer to work and therefore get back on track. Moreover, schools ameliorate some of the most basic aspects of poverty and neglect. The kids are warm and safe in a school.

Alvarez's on-the-ground observations dovetail with those made by Molly McGrath Tierney, the former administrator of a large city agency. When interviewed, Tierney emphasized that "poverty is often confused for neglect. Interventions should be rare and brief." The key, she believes, is to intervene as early as possible, which means figuring out the early warning signs and capitalizing on them immediately. Those signs might include looking at substance abuse findings, noting when children are struggling at school, and picking up on deaths or absences in the family.

These signals come from a variety of sources, including schools, hospitals, utility companies (when bills go unpaid), and homeless shelters. We need a way to integrate how this data is gathered and understood. If that were implemented, then subsidizing rent or directing people to relevant social services could happen before domestic situations become dire. "The idea," Tierney asserts, "is you help get people back on track and the kids stay with them."

Tierney believes that early intervention would produce measurable outcomes: fewer kids in foster care; shorter stays in foster care; better performance in school; lower levels of substance abuse. It would also be possible to demonstrate how much money the government saves as a result of these social improvements.

Is Tierney's scenario of data-driven early intervention plausible? I spoke with Michael O'Connell, chief data scientist at TIBCO, the Silicon Valley company whose software powers data-dependent operations such as FedEx, T-Mobile, and JetBlue.

O'Connell noted that cities are increasingly implementing open data policies. Such open data from municipalities could serve as the basis for alert systems. "If you have data that has a regular refresh rate," O'Connell explains, "you can look for outliers across time." In other words, with a reliable stream of data that's regularly updated, the alert signals become clearer and clearer. That makes neglect situations easier to identify and act on.

Recent advances in technology enable early intervention to go much further. With enough data, it's conceivable that artificial intelligence could be used in *predictive* ways. If a large number of child abuse cases reveals that certain behavioral patterns often lead to neglect or abuse, then we can address problems before things get too bad. Disconcerting behavior patterns might include parent's not paying utility bills combined with a dramatic increase in a child's disciplinary problems at school. Intervention and remedial action could occur before the problems even manifest.

The technology to do this exists now. However, O'Connell warns that to properly develop predictive capabilities, "There would need to be a model that ties early data to longer-term outcomes." He cautioned that it's not an easy problem to solve. Studies would need control groups of "normal" parents and children, for comparison purposes. The next step would be to build an inventory of available data from various agencies, as well as a review of relevant academic literature upon which to base the decision-making capabilities of the computer programs.

That effort is complicated, but we do this kind of work for a wide range of human and natural activities. These include developing pharmaceuticals, stock trading, and weather forecasting. As a society, we are prepared to pay the cost for those activities because we understand the economic benefits, particularly when there's a profit motive involved. If we really understood the costs of foster care, both in economic terms and in human suffering, we could muster the resources to address the problems of child neglect in this manner. We need to make it a priority.

There are also examples of preventative efforts, already underway. These options don't require massive investment in technology, but they would benefit from broader political support.

Casey Family Programs is the eight-hundred-pound gorilla among non-profit organizations that work in child services. It was established in 1966—a year earlier than Downey Side—by Jim Casey, the founder of United Parcel Service. It has $2.4 billion in assets and spends about $125 million a year on its projects. Despite being the reverse image of Downey Side financially, its philosophy is in complete alignment. The foundation sees foster care as the legacy of a century-old punitive attitude toward "morally unfit" families. That old model has been adapted over time to target so-called undeserving groups by "equating child safety with removing the child from his or her family." Casey is opposed to foster care except as a very last resort.

The foundation launched a program called "2020: Building Communities of Hope." Among its goals is "a 50 percent reduction in the need for foster care." As part of this effort, pilot programs have been initiated in several communities around the country. One of these programs is in Alachua County, in north-central Florida, where the city of Gainesville is located.

Florida has a waiver for its federal foster-care funding (Title IV-E) that gives it a measure of flexibility in how the money used. Thus, the state has more freedom to invest in innovative preventative services. In 2007, when the waiver came into effect, Florida had some of the highest rates of child removal, with some zip codes in Alachua County being particularly distressed.

Working with a local community-based agency, Partnership for Strong Families (PSF) and the state Department of Children and Families (DCF), Casey identified the areas that most needed support services. In a novel move, when the Alachua County Library District expressed a desire to open branches in the same areas, a unique approach was born. It's called the Library Partnership.

"As you can understand, people weren't really excited about going to DCF, the place where they take your children, to try and get help when they needed it," explains Ester Tibbs, a former DCF district administrator now on PSF's board. "So, we were looking for a welcoming, non-stigmatized environment that families could come to seeking help."

Since 2012, three library centers have opened in the county. They don't look at all like typical welfare offices. They are real libraries that also offer one-stop shopping for support and preventive services. People can get food, clothing, homework help for children, parenting classes, job-readiness training, and financial literacy courses. Everything is customized to suit the needs of residents in neighborhoods that have experienced high rates of child abuse and neglect.

Over the first six years, the results of this operation have been dramatic. In two of the county's zip codes where the Library Partnership operates, verified maltreatment of children has plunged by between 44 and 58 percent. Removal of children from their families has also fallen considerably while reunification of children with their birth parents has risen correspondingly.

Brother Terry whole heartedly supports the idea of reallocating resources toward supporting families so that foster care is less needed. He has been advocating a long time for that. He also believes we can frame the adoption side of the foster-care equation in a more favorable light.

After decades of toiling at the fault line where foster care meets adoption, Brother Terry offers a fresh take. Even though he works daily with families mired in poverty, he believes the foster-care problem is far less overwhelming than it appears. It's counterproductive, he says, to talk about five hundred thousand kids trapped in the system because it depersonalizes the problem and makes it seem so vast that only big government can deal with it.

This depersonalized view is used to justify the interventionist approach, creating a deplorable loop of negative reinforcement. Meanwhile the real problem—at the core of foster care—is that an abstract entity, the state, is the legal guardian of children rather than flesh and blood parents. "It's like making McDonald's, General Motors, or some other corporation . . . parents," he mused. "How well would that work out? They don't have laps kids can sit on."

Instead, Brother Terry, chipped away at the numbers to come up with a startling revelation. Counterintuitively, he first doubled the number of needy kids by adding in runaways, approximately another five hundred thousand nationwide. However, he believed that 80 percent in foster care, and 50 percent of the runaways could go immediately to a permanent home. That might mean their own nuclear family, extended family, or non-relatives who acted like their family.

This would leave 350,000 children who still needed families. Of these, three quarters had siblings. So, if the sibling groups could go to the same families, that would reduce the number of "placements" to 262,500. Roughly half, 131,250, were traumatized or "troubled" children.

Brother Terry demonstrates that the pool of possible adoptee recipients in the country is eighty-three million self-identified families. This means that a mere 0.3 percent, or three in every one thousand families, would need to adopt a child. About one in every thousand families would need to take in a severely traumatized youth. That's about one family or so per suburb or small town. It doesn't even take a village. It just takes a single villager.

When I fly across the country, I often look down from the plane window and think about what Brother Terry said as I pass over the villages, towns, and cities of America. Which house could be that one home? Is it that place on the corner with the big tree? That one with the red roof? Maybe that apartment over the grocery store? Do the people who live in these homes know they are needed?

Father Paul took a single sixteen-year-old boy, a so-called juvenile delinquent, and found him a home. This one action energized a church group to form a committee, which then galvanized a community. Eventually, the small organization sprouted offices across different states. With very little in the way of resources, Downey Side has found permanent homes for around seven thousand children over the course of a half a century.

I hope that the communities I see from the plane's window will be inspired to do two things: First, give one foster child a permanent home in the community; second, plead with the community's congressperson to change the system so that it empowers families rather than tearing them apart. Just these two changes could bring our national hostage crisis to an end.

What about you? Start by talking about foster care with your friends and neighbors. Tell them what you've learned. Perhaps you'll adopt a child. That's the legacy of Downey Side—to inspire individuals and communities to set America's youngest hostages free.

About this Book

Thumbs Up for Downey Side

Seven years ago, I broke my thumb before the annual Race for Kids, a ski race. I'm embarrassed to say that the accident was more like Charlie Chaplin than James Bond. (Luckily nobody witnessed it.) After I arrived at the local hospital, a priest showed up. I thought, *Jesus, it's just a thumb! I don't need my last rites!*

Father Paul was very gracious and drove me back to the resort. Along the way he told me Downey Side could use a little marketing help. I thought, in my Oxycodone haze, maybe I'd write a brochure for them. A nice, simple three-fold. It would only cost a few hours of my time. Well, that grew into a rebranding effort: building a web site—along with another marketing agency—and helping Downey Side with communications. (Priests … they are uncanny businessmen.)

For the past three years, I've been working with Father Paul on this book. We had hoped to release it for Downey Side's jubilee, but the time passed and we missed the date. However, during the time it's taken to write the book, I've spent hours talking with Father Paul. That time has only increased my admiration for him and his work.

Because of Downey Side's effort, because of the love they have for their parents, thousands of children have been given a better life. With over seven thousand children in placed in permanent families, the fiftieth anniversary was a chance to celebrate its much-deserved success.

However, this book was not written with success in mind. It's about failure.

A child's life is too valuable for us to fail.

The successes of Downey Side emerge from an enormous backdrop of failure called the foster-care system. Downey Side rescues children from this system all across the country.

Today, there are five hundred thousand kids in foster care in the US. A huge number of them are stuck there. Foster care isn't a success. It's a disaster of biblical proportions.

Father Paul has witnessed this failure firsthand for fifty years. He wants to see something new. Foster care as we know it has to be dismantled.

Our book is titled, *America's Youngest Hostages*. That's how we see the kids in foster care—held against their will for ransom.

America's Youngest Hostages transforms Father Paul's rage against the system into a vehicle for change. We hope that you will spread its message as widely as you can.

Acknowledgments

Writing can be a lonely journey, but that has not been the case with this book. My sincere thanks go to the entire Downey Side community, the people who have helped and encouraged me every step of the way. I must also thank the Financial Communications Society for their unflagging interest in this project and their ongoing support to Downey Side.

There are many, many individuals who have made contributions to this effort. First among them is Kimberly Frink. Without Kim this book wouldn't exist. Neither would Downey Side, I suspect. Alongside Kim, Jo Ann Nolan rolled up her sleeves and dived into the research that was crucial to my understanding of foster care and the workings of adoption agencies.

Sister Liz Engel deserves special credit for connecting me to adoptive families and providing endless insights into the byzantine bureaucracy of child welfare. She also generously hosted me while I was researching in New Jersey. Her tireless encouragement is only matched by her boundless commitment to giving kids a better life, a spirit shared by her remarkable volunteer crew on the Jersey Shore.

In Springfield Massachusetts, Marty Pilon welcomed me into her home and into the Pilon family. Through Marty's keen wit, enthusiasm, and ample provision of wine, I was able to imagine what the early days of Downey Side were like and to glimpse hidden facets of Father Paul when he was young priest. Retired Springfield Sheriff Mike Ashe clarified my vision, serving as my tour guide at the original Downey Side group home, which he ran. He also introduced me to its former inhabitants, Jerry Boillat and Jim Minelli, who graciously answered my questions. Jim Tourtelotte helped me understand how the agency came into being and grew. Elliott and Kay Stratton generously recounted the trials, tribulations, and triumphs of house parenting.

Over the years, numerous Downey Side families have shared their adoption experiences with me. I must thank Jason and Natasha Cranston, Diana Bassman, Anna McNamara, Beth Schaefer, Charles and Donna Skee, and Matt Zamot for sharing their fraught emotional journeys.

Brother Terry Taffe shared his deep understanding of child welfare, which comes from years of work in that trench. As a repository of the withering memories of octogenarians, he was able to furnish historical details that would have remained undiscovered. I would be remiss not to single out Todd Broccolo, my companion in arms since we joined forces at the Stowe, Vermont hospital, at the beginning of my involvement with Downey Side.

Numerous people beyond those at Downey Side have broadened my perspective. I must thank the following people for their time, expertise, and understanding: Anita Alvarez, Maris Blechner, Sixto Cancel, April Dinwoodie, Garry Melon, Leora Neal, Michael O'Connell, Degen Pener, Molly McGrath Tierney, Rich Valenza, and Denise Williams.

Special gratitude is owed to Sahara Briscoe, whose unremitting support through the ups and downs of writing has kept me even keeled and focused on completion. Laura Hanifin brought Downey Side's photo album up to printable standards.

My greatest thanks go to Father Paul. What a privilege and inspiration it has been to spend time with him over the past several years. He has gifted me with the understanding of what "grace" truly means.

Lastly, I must thank all the adoptive parents in the country. In a world increasingly short of time, empathy, and understanding, their commitment to permanency is a beacon of hope for us all.

About the Author

Ian Keldoulis

Ian is an Australian writer who prefers shade to sunshine and crowded sidewalks to the outback. His favorite sport isn't cricket or rugby, but people watching. That's good, because he was transplanted to New York City over three decades ago.

Writing has been the one constant in his life, beginning with underground magazines while studying at Sydney University. Then he traveled to Tokyo, and wound up writing for a local production company, Twenty First City, and then went on to do Japanese kid's TV. Some work for PBS and Showtime followed when he moved to New York.

A stint in publishing led to stories in *The New York Times*, *Harper's Bazaar*, and other media outlets before he was lured into advertising, eventually running his own agency and winning ten awards. A period that included a lot of animated dog commercials for Barclays bank.

His involvement with The Financial Communications Society, one of Downey Side's key sponsors, brought him into contact with Father Paul, the priest who appeared at the end of Ian's hospital bed following his accident at an annual charity ski race in Stowe, Vermont. Father Paul declined to administer last rites.

Instead, on the ride back to the resort, he convinced Ian (who at the time was on medication for severe pain) to help with the charity's communications. Ian agreed. He has since helped rebrand Downey Side, create numerous communications pieces, and publish this book.

Father Paul Engel

By Dorothy K. LaMantia, The Monitor, Trenton, NY

"I love families and kids," said Capuchin Franciscan Father Paul Engel, who will celebrate his 50th jubilee of priestly ordination Aug. 17 in Sacred Heart Church, Bay Head, where he has served weekend assistant for the past 27 years.

The anniversary is a milestone for a vocation driven by a passion for family life, rooted in his childhood then blossoming into his life's work.

Born in the Bronx, N.Y., in 1937, Paul Engel was the second of seven children born to Rose and Walter Engel. He spoke of them affectionately, saying "I owe a lot to my family."

A product of Catholic schools, he entered the Capuchin Franciscan friary in 1956, soon after his graduation from Rice High School, Manhattan, which was run by the Christian Brothers.

He entered St. Anthony College, Hudson, N.H., a four-year program affiliated with The Catholic University of America, Washington. After graduating in 1960, he entered Mary Immaculate Seminary in Garrison, N.Y., for theological studies. Ordained a priest Nov. 28, 1964, he was assigned to Our Lady of Sorrows Parish on New York's Lower East Side.

In 1966, he was named assistant chaplain to the Downtown Business Chapel of St. Francis, Springfield, Mass., where his work with youth groups immersed him in the needs of troubled children, who were often homeless after being discharged from foster care.

After much research, Father Engel and three kindred spirits helped launch a mission for homeless children, which eventually became Downey Side.

With its mantra "Kids belong in families, not foster care," Downey Side became the only national adoption agency exclusively devoted to recruiting families for youth seven to 17 years old who need permanent families. The organization finds and prepares families who want to adopt older children, then connects them with older homeless children in the foster-care system.

The program supports the family through the adoption process and beyond. Today the nonprofit, nonsectarian organization has offices in New York, Connecticut, Massachusetts, Minnesota, Missouri, Kansas and New Jersey. The office in Sea Girt is directed by Father Engel's sister, Dominican Sister Elizabeth Engel.

Since its inception, Downey Side has successfully placed over 7,000 children in permanent homes. The average age of adoptees is 12 years.

Father Engel currently spends his weekdays in St. John the Baptist Parish, New York, and heads for Bay Head on the weekends where he celebrates Mass and the Sacraments.

"I love the people there. I am partial to the seniors, being one myself," he joked.

When asked what is most rewarding about his vocation, he said, "I love being free to help people. There is so much joy and life if you help others. God can work with any of us if we let him."

As for his future, he said, "I will take it a year at a time...I am still doing fine, praise God, and I don't want to give up!"

Downey Side

Downey Side is the only national adoption agency exclusively devoted to recruiting families for youth seven- to seventeen-years old who need permanent families. For many children in the foster-care system, adoption is the only safeguard against future homelessness.

Downey Side began in Springfield, Massachusetts in 1967 when Fr. Paul Engel, OFM Cap., a Capuchin priest, placed a seventeen-year-old boy into the home of Margaret Downey.

Thanks to the many devoted parents who chose to make a lifelong commitment to these waiting children, Downey Side has placed over seven thousand youth into permanent adoptive families.

Downey Side's philosophy is rooted in the conviction that every child has the right to a permanent family. It is our purpose to work in partnership with the government as a licensed adoption agency. Down Side is determined to place America's waiting children in permanent homes. We are dedicated to family life for all children, and we strongly believe that a healthy permanent relationship is the best prevention against homelessness.

Downey Side has the additional purpose of leading members of each community to become advocates for children in need.

Downney Side Album

Father Paul and Brian Champoux, the first Downey Side child, also a Capuchin friar.

Father Paul as a young priest in 1956.

Margaret Downey and Father Paul, 1991.

Paul Doherty, Father Paul Engel and Jim Tourtelotte,
founders of Downey Side, several decades later.

Father Paul and the First Downey Side employees, 1971.

Father Paul saying a Mass in a barn in Springfield, MA.

The early days of Downey Side's group homes, Father Paul and youngsters.

Downey Side

On the side of FOSTER KIDS
seeking FOREVER FAMILIES

For over fifty years, Downey Side has been helping older children, sibling groups, and children with special needs find permanent, loving homes.

All proceeds from the sale of this book go to Downey Side.

To learn more about Downey Side and to support its mission please visit **www.downeyside.org**.

CPSIA information can be obtained
at www.ICGtesting.com
Printed in the USA
FFHW022151060819
54138984-59827FF